Kingsley Aikins   Ca

Dharmatilleke   Alex |

Kerry Howard   Vicky   l

MacDonald Ben Newsome Debbie Small Glori

Tabi Annamaria Zuffo Kingsley Aikins Carrie

Benedet   Sahan Dharmatilleke   Alex Blake

Sonya Furlong Kerry Howard Vicky Jamieson

Margaret MacDonald Ben Newsome   Debbie

Small Gloria Tabi Annamaria Zuffo Kingsley

Aikins Carrie Benedet Sahan Dharmatilleke

Alex Blake   Sonya Furlong   Kerry Howard

Vicky Jamieson   Margaret MacDonald   Ben

Newsome Debbie Small Gloria Tabi Annamaria

Zuffo Kingsley Aikins Carrie Benedet Sahan

Dharmatilleke   Alex Blake   Sonya Furlong

Kerry Howard   Vicky Jamieson   Margaret

MacDonald   Ben Newsome   Debbie Small

Gloria Tabi Annamaria Zuffo Kingsley Aikins

Carrie Benedet Sahan Dharmatilleke   Alex

Blake Sonya Furlong Kerry Howard Vicky

Jamieson Margaret MacDonald Ben Newsome

Debbie Small   Gloria Tabi   Annamaria Zuffo

an
g
t

GLOBAL MATTERS

Inspirational stories from leaders influencing the future of culture, business and education.

Created by
CARRIE BENEDET

ed by the Power Writers Publishing Group in 2023.

SBN:978-0-6458010-6-4

A catalogue record for this
book is available from the
National Library of Australia

NATIONAL
LIBRARY
OF AUSTRALIA

Cover design by Miriam Rudolph.

Internal layout by Andrew Davies.

Disclaimer

Any opinions expressed in this work are exclusively those of the
author and are not necessarily the views held or endorsed by others
quoted throughout. All of the information, exercises and concepts
contained within the publication are intended for general information
only. The author does not take any responsibility for any choices that
any individual or organization may make relating to this information in
the business, personal, financial, familial, or other areas of life. If any
individual or organization does wish to implement the ideas discussed
herein, it is recommended that they obtain their own independent
advice specific to their circumstances.

Acknowledgement

I want to acknowledge the traditional custodians of country throughout
Australia and Papua New Guinea and recognise their continuing
connection to land, waters and community. I pay my respects to them
and their cultures, and to Elders both past and present.

CONTENTS

PREFACE

People matter. Thriving matters. Leadership matters. A global focus matters.

It is wonderful that you have our ground-breaking anthology in your hand!

I feel so privileged to have been in the position to bring together this group of like-minded authors who are making a difference at both the individual and collective level in a way that will positively impact our global future.

Over the last four years we have witnessed immense change and there are no signs of the changing landscape settling any time soon. This has brought about the need for a new playbook of global leadership across the fields of culture, business and education. The authors in this book have answered the call to offer their own inspirational stories from their past experiences with a future focused lens. Our genuine hope is that each chapter will inspire and challenge you to live your best life no matter what your circumstances are, with the view to leaning into your leadership wherever you are and wherever you live, love, work, and play.

As you'll be reading in my chapter, I walked the Kokoda Trail for my 50th birthday. Challenging myself in that way changed the trajectory of my life. I am now on a quest to bring together people who are doing extraordinary things in life and work to inspire others who are finding the current conditions challenging. Collectively, human-centred leaders like you and I and so many others are being called to lean into their ability to lead and influence, to spread the word about all the ways we are connected in the interest of making the world a more inclusive place. This mission is especially important in this era of heightened technology and divisive forces that cloud the collective nature of what it is to be human.

I've loved pulling this book together, and I'm really excited to see the ripple effect of showcasing all the ways the authors involved have thrived through adversity and gone on to make a difference.

Even if only one chapter of this book (or part thereof) speaks to you, I hope you will take that as a sign that by sharing your leadership story, you will also be able to influence humanity's response in the face of rapid change as part of the collective voices speaking out against closed hearts and small mindedness.

A deep thank you goes out from the bottom of my heart to Kingsley Aikins, Sahan Dharmatilleke, Alex Blake, Sonya Furlong, Kerry Howard, Vicky Jamieson, Margaret MacDonald, Ben Newsome, Gloria Tabi, Debbie Small, and Annamaria Zuffo. Their chapters are both powerful and modest, and they speak directly to the ethos of the collective power of people with good intentions and open minds.

Together we have the power to create a groundswell around this anthology and its message of hope, leadership, and empowerment.

Let's give it a red hot shot!

CHAPTER ONE

The Power of Networking

Kingsley Aikins

Kingsley Aikins is the founder and CEO of 'The Networking Institute (TNI)' based in Dublin and he and his team run training courses, online and face to face, for individuals, corporates, governments, and academic institutions in the areas of Networking, Philanthropy, Diaspora Engagement and Public Speaking. Prior to establishing TNI he was the worldwide CEO of 'The Ireland Funds', a philanthropic foundation based in Boston, USA, that has raised over $600 million for projects in Ireland. Before that he spent 7 years in Sydney, Australia representing 'Enterprise Ireland' and 'IDA Ireland' promoting trade and investment.

You can contact Kingsley at
www.thenetworkinginstitute.com
linkedin.com/in/kingsleyaikins

I am delighted to have the opportunity of writing about something I am very passionate about. That is the power of networking. My background includes spending over 20 years working in 6 countries, and in many of those countries I didn't know anybody when I arrived. So I quickly learnt that to survive and thrive I needed to build a strong and diverse network. I soon realised that this wasn't a luxury, but a necessity. I was also conscious about the number one predictor of career success which is to have an open network rather than a closed one. So I got busy with building an open network with a wide array of diverse people in it.

In those early days of my career, I learnt some key lessons that helped me enormously as my career progressed. Firstly, I realised that there are two types of Networks. The first one is an organic network which is a function of being a part of a family where you grow up, the school or college you go to and the sports and hobbies that you have. The thing is that you don't actively go out and build this kind of network – it just happens. But as I got going in my career and became a manager, I grew to appreciate the fact that I needed to tap into another type of network that was more intentional and strategic.

What I realised as my career progressed was that while the skills I needed to get my job in the first instance were critically important, they became less important as time went on. I say that because everyone I worked with had more or less the same skills as I did, so those skills didn't provide me with a competitive edge of any kind. However, the competitive edge I managed to develop revolved around the power of relationships. I feel like it's a shame that so many people miss that important inflection point.

The other thing I realised early on in my career was that perhaps the formal education structures of schools and colleges are partly to blame for this. You see, progress in these institutions is a function of getting a mark, a grade, a score or whatever, while having nothing to do with the people skills we develop in the context of interacting with those around us. So, notwithstanding the roles where particular qualifications are required, when we get into the real world of work there are a whole range of so-called soft skills and qualities we require to be able to effectively interact with others.

What I'm referring to here are things like our attitude in general, and the qualities of determination, resilience, empathy, grit, and humour that we bring with us when we turn up at work. These are the things that make the difference when it comes to the impact we can have. These are some of the unwritten rules of career progress these days that can't be measured. And yet they are enormously impactful and influential.

The third really valuable thing I learnt about in the process of establishing myself as a networking specialist was the importance of taking what I call the ATM approach. I call it that because the way some people network reminds me of the consequences of going to the ATM machine and continually taking money out without ever making any deposits. In the case of an actual ATM machine, sooner or later we'll be greeted by a flashing sign that says 'Insufficient Funds' if we're not careful. Similarly, if we keep trying to get things from our network without giving as much or even more back to the people in it, it's unlikely to be sustainable over the long run. You see, networking is a two-way reciprocal process where the more you give, the more you get.

The other thing I noticed as I was networking in the early days, was that the world is full of great ideas, but many of them are never realised. That's a shame because when ideas are in people's heads they can't be found on Google or anywhere else for that matter. Whereas when they are shared with others the sky's really the limit. This is where networking really comes into its own because the conversations people have within their networks provides a rich source of ideas, suggestions, advice, tips, and even gossip.

One of the hidden and enduring costs of Covid is that our networks shrunk. We got comfortable hunkering down with friends, family and just a few business connections, preferring to stay within the inner concentric ring of our network where we have strong emotional bonds. I want to put it to you that ignoring the outer concentric ring where we have a wide array of weaker ties represents a lost opportunity. I say that because engaging with both the inner and outer rings and beyond is where we can collectively have the most impact.

As I review the outcomes of the first couple of years where we increasingly got to understand that Covid was here to stay in one way or another, it seems to me that there has been less business development, less learning on the job, less randomness and serendipity, and less fun. Or as we say in Ireland, there has been less craic. What's more, I feel like people are less loyal to their companies, and a positive company culture is more difficult to develop and sustain these days.

So, from where I sit, the time is right for us to take on the challenge of refreshing our existing networks as well as building new ones. Or if you're not a networker yet, I recommend you get started.

Previously it felt like our lives were permanent and predictable. Now there's no denying that we are living in a rapidly changing world where technology and globalisation are wiping out whole industries, and software driven disruption is the norm. The environment we're living in now is sometimes described using the acronym VUCA. This acronym stands for volatility, uncertainty, complexity, and ambiguity. This certainly rings true to me because new technologies, AI, data analytics and social networks are having a huge impact on how we communicate, collaborate and work. The one certainty to note is that we will all be facing a bewildering array of challenging changes in the future. That's why I recommend connecting with a network or networks to help you navigate the options available for you to make the most of changing circumstances.

The bottom line is that networking is an important 'soft' skill. In my opinion, these days it's right up there with the more traditional soft skills like teamwork, communication, and critical thinking – all of which are becoming more important than ever. One of the many advantages of having these soft skills is that they are hard to automate. In other words, as computers are poor at replacing humans when it comes to the generative impact of interaction and collaboration, honing your people skills and getting good at networking is a great way to future-proof your career.

I'd encourage you to see your network as not just a safety net you can call on when things go wrong and you need help, but also as a trampoline that will bounce you into new opportunities. In that sense, networking is a critical business and career building tool. I say that because the old idea that working hard and playing by the rules to get ahead is no longer enough. The key to success these days includes working harder, and regularly reinventing and educating ourselves through lifelong learning. These are the new rules we need to play by. I say that because traditional lifetime career structures are a thing of the past. The typical escalator model of career progress where you join a company at a young age and work your way up to the corner office is gone forever.

Companies outlived people back in the day, but now people outlive companies. In fact, the average company only lasts about 20 years now, and the average executive in a C suite position lasts about 7 years. What this means is that we need to be constantly thinking about how to position ourselves to get the next job. This is where having a solid network is critical when it comes to developing our own career 'playbook'. Essentially, intelligent networking has become a career lubricant and career accelerator.

I trust I've convinced you of the reason you should be considering networking by now, so as the space I have here is limited, I'm going to share some of the key insights I've drawn in relation to the way things are done by successful people now that will help you to thrive.

Life is a game of inches: The difference between winning and losing can be tiny. While on the one hand we're talking about something that is minuscule, the implications are anything but. In fact, they can be enormous. We see this playing out in sport all the time. A great example relates to David Brailsford who took over the running of British cycling after a century of the team having won virtually nothing. Things changed when he introduced the notion of marginal gains. The idea of marginal gains is that being 1% better than the opposition often doesn't only get you 1% ahead. In fact, it can actually get you a whole lot more, much the same as being 1% worse doesn't get you 1% less. The bad news is that it can often get you nothing.

What Brailsford did was break down the act of cycling into every single element and worked on continually improving each element by 1%. The results of this approach were seriously impressive with the team taking home dozens of medals from the Olympics and going on to win the Tour de France six times by applying the same principles. So, the lesson in this for you is that if you look to improve everything you do by 1%, the cumulative effect adds up to a much more substantial improvement than you might imagine.

One introduction leading to one conversation can change your life: This point is not unrelated to the previous one, but it narrows in on the value of person to person contact and the fact that immense opportunities can come out of the simplest of conversations. The thing is that these types of conversations don't happen when you're lying in bed or sitting at your desk. They happen when you are out and about, changing your routines, talking to strangers, seeking out different sorts of people, putting your talents on display, speaking and presenting all over the place, and building an online tribe.

Nobody started a large organisation: Everything starts at zero. For example, the 21-year-old son of a Syrian migrant Steve Jobs and 27-year-old Steve Wozniak got started in a garage in Cupertino, California where they produced the first Apple computer. Around the corner in a shed Bill Hewlett and David Packard started their printer company with $500. Not far away, Walt Disney produced the first cartoon in a garage. Household names like Facebook, Amazon and Starbucks started in peoples' bedrooms. Ryanair started with one plane and 18 passengers they flew from Waterford in Ireland to London in 1985. Now they fly 20 million passengers a month. All these companies had very modest beginnings and went on to be major successes.

The moral in these examples is that you can make something big out of very modest beginnings, but you can't do it alone. The way to do it is to network your way to success. This involves rejecting the myth of individualism and the notion that success is all about the rugged individual taking on the world on their own. The truth is that no matter how brilliant you are, if you are playing a solo game, you will always lose to a team.

People need to interact with other people to thrive: Opportunities don't float around on clouds. They are attached to people. So, if you are looking for an opportunity, what you are really looking for is a person. That's why I say that the best way to gather great information and access that elusive spark of creativity is to talk to people in your network. The thing is that everybody you ever met knows somebody you don't know, and the way to get to people you don't know is through people you do know.

Reid Hoffman who is the co-founder of LinkedIn has written extensively on this topic. He advises companies to invest in the power of people working together by creating network intelligence programmes. Hoffman's argument is based on a very simple premise. It is that there are more smart people outside the company in question than inside of it. Network intelligence provides access to these people and the knowledge they hold (which is often not publicly available). The key then is to build enough trust so that your employees are willing to use their networks on behalf of the company.

To summarise, networking is about building long term sustainable relationships where people (including you) are involved with their hearts and minds. Most people agree with that definition. However not everybody agrees with the next bit that I see as integral to the effectiveness of networking. That is, that networking is essentially about giving not getting. If you take that approach, I'm confident networking will enable you to take your success to a whole other level.

CHAPTER TWO

Give Me Your Hand
– Let's Take This Journey Together

Carrie Benedet

Carrie Benedet is an education specialist and leadership coach who focuses on both personal and professional growth mindsets with aspiring and experienced leaders and teams in education systems, government, and business. She is an advocate of 'human – centred leaders' with 24 years of industry experience in creating, leading and hosting leadership experiences, programs and courses, both face to face and virtually. She infuses strong emotional intelligence and relational leadership skills to empower a culture of respect and engagement in workplace relationships, within teams and across organisations. Carrie's skills lie in her ability to connect across cultures and challenge current attitudes and behaviours of stakeholders to develop well rounded future leaders and teams. Carrie is a global speaker, author, mentor, coach, podcast host, and the designer and facilitator of retreat and immersion experiences.

You can contact Carrie at
linkedin.com/in/carriebenedet
www.carriebenedet.com

Are you sceptical whenever you see someone reach out their hand and say, "Give me your hand"? Do you step backwards? Do you hear yourself say, "Leave me alone, I can do it by myself"?

That's what I used to be like. My past is littered with times when I've put on my 'I can do it myself' mask. Quite often I added in a dismissive attitude and/or a bit of belligerence in the process of proving that I didn't need anybody's help. These days I'm very grateful for the type of self-awareness that enables me to share these things with you. I say that because while I'm sharing my story with you here, this book isn't about me. It's about you. If there's one thing I know for sure after spending six decades on this planet, it's that we're all in this together.

The thing is that there comes a time when taking that 'hand' someone offers you can mean the difference between life and death. It can be the turning point where action trumps inertia, and being stuck in a pattern of blame transitions into a new perspective leading to the solution of a problem that might have seemed unsolvable before.

Take a moment to think about which approach you usually take.

What I know now is that when we have no choice, we'll take the offer of help that is extended.

Let me share a story with you about how getting down and dirty in the trenches led to my leaning into a space of true self-leadership on the Kokoda Trail in Papua New Guinea.

By way of background, I have never thought of myself as anything special or out of the ordinary. Basically, I did what was expected of me growing up as the oldest of six siblings in a small country town in NSW. I got married straight out of Teachers College and started having children more or less immediately. So, when a significant birthday arrived (and I'm talking fifty years' worth of celebration here) I decided it was time for me to shake things up a bit. I felt like I needed a long hard trek of some kind to work a few things out because life as I knew it, where my focus was on bringing up our four beautiful children was rapidly transitioning as they were having children of their own.

So, I found myself at a crossroads. The question I needed to be able to answer for myself was – where do I fit in under these new circumstances? Or to put that another way – who am I now?

Looking back over my early days of parenting, it's clear that I was a self-starter who spent a decade at home making extra money designing and sewing fashion when home loan interest rates were sky high at 17.5%. I actually did quite well out of that while the 'liquorice allsorts' (as we affectionately call our kids) were at school. I also put myself forward for a number of voluntary parent leadership roles at local, regional and state levels in New South Wales where I'm based. This laid the foundations for a successful career with Sydney Catholic Education that spanned some 23 years. I cherish the mentors and colleagues I had the privilege of working alongside back in those days.

But that was then, and what I decided to do to find out who I was when being a mum had become much less hands on than it had ever been before, was to really challenge myself

GIVE ME YOUR HAND

on all levels by walking the Kokoda Trail. What attracted me to walking one of the most arduous trails in the world was a desire to give thanks for being able to bring my family up in a free country like Australia.

The contrast couldn't have been starker. The Kokoda Trail was the setting of one of the most brutal military battles during World War II. It was there, some 81 years ago, where thousands of Australian, American, and local Papua New Guinean men fought and died in a series of gruelling clashes against the advancing Japanese Army. Today, many wartime artefacts remain virtually undisturbed in the forests of Papua New Guinea. Trekkers are likely to stumble on anything from unused mortars and grenades, to discarded helmets and army boots, and even the remains of a US P40 Kittyhawk fighter plane which is still in situ.

That said, I realise you might still be wondering why I decided to explore my future life options through taking on what is known as the world's most difficult trekking challenge. That's a reasonable question because I had never done anything like this before. I'd never even camped out to be honest. Yet I had chosen to do a trek that involved roughly 158 kilometres climbing 6,750 metres over 8 days spent in humid jungles and torrential terrain. In other words, I had chosen to subject myself to conditions that would stretch the mental and physical limits of even the toughest among us.

Needless to say, trekking up, over, and down the Owen Stanley Ranges was quite a feat for a 50-year-old woman who had more or less focussed on the development of the grey matter in her head (rather than her abilities in the way of physical strength and endurance) up until a few months before the departure date.

Looking back on it now, trekking the Kokoda Trail was the most momentous thing I have ever done in my life. In saying that, I don't want to downplay the incredible experience of doing life with my partner Luc and parenting our four precious children together. That said, I have to give myself credit for embarking on the challenge without a buddy. Just before leaving Sydney for Port Moresby, my daughter Cara hugged me and said, "Mum, you know there's no shame in having to come home before you get to Kokoda." Little did she know how much of an incentive she provided me with when she said those words. By the way, most of my family thought I had rocks in my head.

I felt a huge imperative to complete the trek and I knew I would need to do a lot of work on myself to get ready. So I started the preparation of my body and mind with Nicole Katrib who I took on as my trainer. I look back on our training sessions with such gratitude for her total belief in me. We probably should have started six months earlier, but hindsight can be a pain in the proverbial, and as they say in the classics – better late than never. Our goal was simple. It was for me to make it all the way and come home in one piece. Little did I know the experience was going to deliver so much more than that.

That last sentence brings me to the point of sharing a transformational afternoon in the wilderness when I heard a booming voice say, "Give me your hand." It seems like an understatement to say that this was a pivotal moment in my life.

It happened about three days into the trek as we were making our way along the Imita Ridge towards Kokoda. Unseasonal monsoonal rain had been relentless all day. I was a bit slower than the other 29 trekkers, so Jobson who was my porter, and Joe the foreman, and another one of the porters had been hanging back with me all day. At one stage I lost my footing and started to slide down the side of the ridge. I couldn't see clearly or find anything to grab hold of, so I continued to slide until I managed to wrap my legs around a thin rubber tree trunk. Shaking and terrified, I knew the only way out of the predicament I was in was to let go of the trunk and take the enormous hand that was reaching out to me.

This was literally one of those life and death situations we usually only hear about, so I had to draw on my capacity to trust, and in spite of the instinct to hang on for dear life, I had to let go of the rubber tree so that I could be pulled up the ridge to safety. In order to do that, I had to park my terror, calm myself down, and concentrate on listening to the instructions I was being given. All the while, images of my beautiful family kept crossing my mind as time seemed to stand still. I had to fully put my trust in the people who were ready to work together with me to get me out of danger. We didn't really know each other at the time, but we understood that each of us needed each other. It was as if there was a silent pact bringing out the deep care we all had for humanity whilst honouring the lives lost in the pursuit of freedom in that special place we were in.

I learnt a lot about myself that day!

That evening we walked into camp many hours after everyone else. We were totally saturated and shaking uncontrollably as we were greeted with an incredible welcome including warm food and people rallying around to help us get dry. Basically, my survival was the result of an incredible team effort. Among other things, that night Charlie Lynn who was the head of the trek gave me his dry tent to sleep in, and he wouldn't take no for an answer.

Looking back on it now, I can say that while they weren't all as dramatic as the third day was, each day was a quest in itself. While I was walking along the ridge that nearly did me in, I had time to think, scream, and accept tears of joy and pain in the way cathartic experiences like the one I had on that ridge are good at opening us up to.

As a group, we all naturally fell into different roles throughout the trek, with things that needed to be done like triaging blisters, stings, cuts, and sprains, as well as sharing ointments and spare painkillers, all getting done one way or another. To be part of this collective spirit was amazing. I found it truly humbling watching people I didn't know accept each other as equal parts of the team while leaning in to care for each other and share the responsibilities for doing what we needed to do to get through each day. This was absolutely the space I needed to be in at the time. It was quite simple really. We all shared a common pursuit while we selflessly helped and valued each other.

Five of our group of thirty were airlifted out for a variety of reasons including a broken patella, a broken ankle, cellulitis, and another trekker walked for four days with a dislocated shoulder. I came home with seven toenails in various stages of disrepair (that all fell off in the end); no skin on both heels; and deep purple bruises on my thighs and buttock, as well as an intestinal parasite that was giving many of us grief at both ends if you know what I mean.

Every village and campsite we trekked through and camped at had a significant story for us to hear. We were privileged to have the opportunity to get to know the chiefs and villagers including the mums with young babies and children everywhere we stopped. We loved immersing ourselves in their culture and getting to understand the health and equity challenges they faced on a day-to-day basis.

As I limped into the camp at Isurava on about the fifth afternoon, I passed the boulder where Victoria Cross recipient Private Bruce Steel Kingsbury of 2/14 Battalion is honoured for his actions at Isurava on 29 August 1942. What a levelling experience that was for me. His selflessness and courage forced me to put the excruciating pain and worrying state of my toenails into a whole other perspective. To this day I can't imagine how on earth those brave soldiers endured such cruel conditions.

After making camp and changing into something clean while tending to my toes, I went exploring this particularly significant camp site. I was genuinely overcome as I slid down through more mud towards the memorial that honours all the other Australian and Papua New Guinean soldiers.

I needed to take more than a moment there. It was as if something held me. I felt transported in time and incredibly privileged being there in silence, and able to give thanks for all I had in my life. It was totally overwhelming and intimate.

A sense of calm descended over me. I had a deep sense of being one with the world on sacred ground, and I could feel the peace of a place that now honoured humankind for their sacrifice. I say this openly in honour of all of the lives sacrificed by Australia, America, and Papua New Guinea.

I realised I was having a 'spiritual experience' when an even deeper sense of calm descended as I came to a stunning clearing that looked straight down the valley we had trudged our way through. The memorial before me featured four black granite pillars, each inscribed with a single word – 'courage', 'endurance', 'mateship', and 'sacrifice'. These words represented the values and qualities of the Australian and allied soldiers who fought along the trail. There really isn't an adequate word to express the feeling I had when I encountered this memorial, suffice to say that the enormity of the meaning of the single words engraved in the granite was incredibly poignant.

Going on a trek like this with the level of emotional and physical challenge it entails opens up plenty of time to reflect deeply on what we tell ourselves about who we are. It allows the luxury of time and space to lean into questions around how we stay true to our values and beliefs, and make sure that our assumptions don't limit our ability to live our best life.

This experience was so profound that it literally changed the trajectory of my life.

As I was walking into Kokoda Village on the final day of the trek Jobson said, "Carrie, they're talking about you. They say you are one strong woman because you shouldn't have made it." I was taken aback because I had never thought of myself that way, but at the same time, everything felt very different after surviving my experience on the ridge and the state I was in when I came across the granite pillars. To tell you the truth, I remember feeling exhausted and ecstatic at the same time. Basically, the challenges I faced on that trek enabled me to become acquainted with the strong side of myself I had never really connected with before.

Courage, mateship, endurance, and sacrifice are values and behaviours I witnessed in action every day on the trail. I also recognise and deeply admire these values in the day to day lives of my family, friends, workmates, and the broader connections I have across the globe. This mindset of leading with confidence and empathy is core to our human-centred approach to leadership. Basically, the pillars that guide us through the mess of life, and the grit and grace of humanity to strive and thrive in adversity is phenomenal.

Leaving my blood-stained boots behind for the local porters to share when they accompanied the next group of trekkers, I flew back over the trail we had walked for eight days, feeling a little lighter in body and soul. I actually 'star jumped' off the plane when it landed back in Port Moresby because I was stunned that I made it back pretty much in one piece when five others had to be airlifted out. Why? Among other things, I realised just how much my mental tenacity had triumphed over my physical fitness and the challenges I encountered. I was amazed, and just so grateful for being part of something that was so life changing.

When I look back on the time we spent trudging through the jungle, soaked to the bone from either torrential rain or body sweat most days, it is clear to me that every person has the capacity to become more than they think they are.

As the world alters dramatically while being propelled onwards by the speed of technology, the four pillars talk to the relationship we have with ourselves and others. They remind us to be mindful of the choices we make, and of the importance of regularly checking in with our values, beliefs, and assumptions. They also beckon us to ask three important questions. They are –

- What kind of leadership do we need for an uncertain future?
- Will we take up the challenge to put humanity first?
- How will we regularly step into our 'Kokoda' to thrive, not just survive?

I want to extend my hand to you aspiring and experienced human-centred leaders who can spread the word about all the ways we are connected in the interest of making the world a more inclusive place where everyone has an opportunity to thrive.

CHAPTER THREE

Discovering Inner Wisdom
– A Journey from Chaos to Clarity

Sahan Dharmatilleke

Sahan Dharmatilleke is the Founder of 'Resilience Within Consultants' and 'YesWeCan.LK'. He specializes in providing neuroscience-based tools and techniques for cultivating Mindfulness, Resilience, and Emotional Intelligence. Sahan has trained over 10,000 participants from 30+ countries, including Healthcare Professionals, Corporate Leaders, Academics, Social Workers, Prisoners, and Cancer Patients. He holds an MA in Psychotherapy, MSc. in Business Psychology, MBA (UK), and B.B.Mgt (1st Class). He is also the first Sri Lankan to hold the distinction of being a faculty member for the Google-born 'Search Inside Yourself Leadership Institute'. Currently, he is working on promoting wellbeing among university students through a free wellbeing platform called 'YesWeCan.LK'.

You can contact Sahan at
www.rwithin.com and www.yeswecan.lk
www.linkedin.com/in/sahan-d/

I t was an ordinary day at work with the usual flurry of activity and the monotony of my routine playing out. But in an instant, the tranquillity was shattered by the shrill sound of a phone ringing. Little did I know that this seemingly ordinary event would become a pivotal moment that would alter my perception of life forever.

As my colleague answered the call her face contorted into a look of anguish. Then her voice started quivering with pain and disbelief as she absorbed the devastating news the caller was delivering. The voice on the other end of the line carried the weight of distress and desperation that was generated by the heart-wrenching message it imparted. That message related to the fact that my colleague's daughter had been involved in a serious accident and was in hospital vacillating precariously between life and death.

I stood there as a silent witness to this unfolding tragedy while the enormity of the moment engulfed me. Time seemed to stand still as I observed the anguished expression etched on my colleague's face. It was a poignant reflection of a mother's profound love that was torn between hope and despair. In that moment, the fragility of life, the unpredictability of fate, and the depth of human vulnerability crystallised before my eyes.

This was a stark reminder of the fact that amidst the hustle and bustle of our daily lives, there are moments that pierce through the mundane fabric of the average day and force us to confront the fragility of our mortal existence. The veil of complacency was literally lifted from my eyes as I witnessed the agony of a mother facing the unthinkable possibility of losing her precious child.

Finding Wisdom Amidst Chaos

The events of the day replayed in my mind like a movie stirring a whirlwind of thoughts and reflections as I drove home from work. The stark reality of our existence washed over me, revealing a profound truth that seems to elude our relentless pursuit of knowledge and education. I say that because in spite of the vast reservoirs of information we accumulate, we often find ourselves ill-equipped to navigate the inevitable challenges that life presents.

I pondered the complexities of human existence during that solitary drive home. I reflected on the fact that while we invest years in our education, diligently acquiring knowledge in a myriad of subjects, from mathematics to science, and economics to politics, we're likely to discover a disconcerting void within us when we're faced with the profound trials life inevitably throws our way. These could be anything from failed relationships, debilitating illnesses, and/or the shadow of mortality.

For those who are able to stay present and resist the option of resorting to strategies that numb the pain, it becomes clear that the knowledge we amassed through textbooks and lectures does little to prepare us for the emotional and psychological toll of the hardships we encounter as we move through our life. In the face of adversity, it can feel as if we're adrift, grappling with a sense of inadequacy because we lack the necessary tools and wisdom to navigate the depths of human experience.

The reality is that even those who continue to 'work' on themselves can still struggle to find the kind of emotional resilience, psychological fortitude, and inner strength required to face the trials of life with grace, wisdom, and equanimity.

This realisation ignited an important question that resulted in my delving into the depths of my soul. The profound period of self-inquiry that followed would forever shape the course of my life. The question that opened that door for me was –

If I only had six months to live, who would I aspire to be, and how would I choose to spend my remaining time?

Universal Truths Unveiled

Fuelled by an insatiable curiosity and an unwavering commitment to understand the depths of the human experience, I embarked on a quest to explore other people's answers to this profound question that had awakened an aspiration to know more within me. So, I sought out people from a diverse range of backgrounds including prisoners on death row to influential CEOs, and others battling the arduous challenges of chemotherapy.

What unfolded during the conversations I had with these people was nothing short of remarkable. An overwhelming 99.9% of the responses echoed a number of common themes. This was an undeniable recognition of the profound human yearnings that lay within us all, and a unique opportunity to access the essence of what truly matters.

The first theme that emerged from these conversations was an innate yearning for philanthropy. People expressed a deep desire to make a positive impact by contributing to the wellbeing of others and the greater good of society. In the face of their own mortality, the pursuit of personal success and material possessions paled into insignificance in comparison to the profound fulfilment that comes from selflessly giving and leaving a lasting legacy of kindness and compassion.

Another prevailing theme that emerged was the deep desire to connect authentically and deeply with loved ones. The value of relationships, of forging meaningful bonds with family, friends, and those dear to us, resonated throughout each conversation I had in the quest to get to the core of what it means to be human. The bottom line is that when confronted with limited time, or shocked into a heightened state of awareness like my colleague was when she answered the call about her daughter's accident, the genuine love and shared experiences that rise to awareness become paramount, outshining the superficial pursuits that usually occupy our daily lives.

Letting go of grievances and embracing forgiveness was another thing that emerged as a transformative and liberating force in the face of mortality. When confronted with the reality of the brevity of life, the weight of grudges and resentments dissipate and become irrelevant. I heard several stories from Individuals who recognised that forgiveness and compassion not only healed relationships, but also freed their heart and mind in a way that enabled inner peace and personal growth to take place.

Lastly, a newfound hunger for spirituality of some kind permeated these conversations. When faced with the finite nature of existence, individuals talked about seeking solace and meaning in the realm of the spiritual. Many expressed a yearning to explore their own spiritual beliefs, to connect with something greater than themselves, and to find comfort and guidance in the realms of faith, prayer, or meditation.

This quest for spiritual nourishment spoke to a deeper understanding of the interconnectedness of all beings and the transcendent nature of the human experience.

Through gathering these insights from a wide range of people, several characteristics emerged in those who became more purposeful, grounded, and fulfilled after being confronted with the prospect of limited time. In summary, the characteristics in question include:

- The pursuit of philanthropy
- The cultivation of deep and authentic connections
- The act of letting go and embracing forgiveness
- The hunger for spiritual nourishment.

It's as if our priorities crystallise and the essence of what really matters comes into sharp focus in these moments of truth and the time after those moments where we process the feelings that emerge. Through that state, differences of opinion converge as universal aspirations that transcend societal divisions and personal backgrounds.

A Life Transformed Through a Mini-Revolution

That day which is forever etched in my memory became a pivotal moment that propelled me into action. It was a catalyst for profound transformation in my own life, and a deep commitment to making a positive impact on society. Fuelled by the insights gained from witnessing the fragility of life and the shared aspirations expressed by individuals facing their mortality, I embarked on a mission to translate those insights into tangible strategies to help people change their focus with the view to creating a ripple effect that would extend far beyond my own existence.

To that end, I went on to launch various initiatives that sought to address the pressing needs of different segments of society. Guided by a deep sense of purpose, I initiated prison programs aimed at providing transformative experiences for individuals on death row as well as those with life sentences. Through these programs, I introduced mindfulness and emotional intelligence practices that empowered incarcerated individuals to cultivate resilience, self-awareness, and a path toward personal growth and rehabilitation.

Recognising the challenges faced by university students in navigating the complexities of their existence while maintaining mental health and wellbeing in an uncertain world, I spearheaded wellbeing initiatives that were aimed at fostering a supportive and nurturing environment on campus. These initiatives offered resources, workshops, and tools for stress management, emotional wellbeing, and personal development to empower young minds to thrive academically, emotionally, and socially.

In my relentless pursuit of creating a meaningful impact, I established a consultancy firm called 'Resilience Within Mental Wellbeing Consultants' that operates with a powerful ethos. A significant portion of our income (25%, to be exact) is dedicated to supporting philanthropic endeavours that address pressing social issues. This commitment ensures our work goes beyond profits and encompasses a deep-rooted sense of responsibility toward the betterment of society.

Through pro-bono workshops and initiatives, we extended our reach and touched the lives of thousands of individuals. Among them were cancer patients for whom we offered pain management programs that combined mindfulness techniques with stress management. Also, in collaboration with peace builders, we conducted workshops on mindfulness, resilience, and emotional intelligence, equipping attendees with invaluable skills to promote harmony and understanding in their communities. Additionally, we offered stress management and resilience building programs to the public, addressing the unique challenges that emerged in the aftermath of the Covid-19 pandemic in particular.

These endeavours were not mere gestures, but intentional efforts to create positive change of a tangible and meaningful nature. They were born out of a deep understanding that transformational impact requires action, not just words. By extending our knowledge, resources, and expertise to those in need, we sought to uplift individuals, empower communities, and foster a more compassionate and resilient society.

The impact of these initiatives goes far beyond numbers and statistics. It resonates within the lives of those touched by our programs. This includes the incarcerated individuals who rediscover hope; the university students who find solace and support; the cancer patients who learn to manage their pain; the peace builders who cultivate understanding; and the people navigating the challenges of a post-pandemic world. Each life that was transformed and each heart we touched represents a testament to the power of collective action and the potential for positive change.

As I reflect on the transformative journey that unfolded from that fateful day, I am humbled and inspired by the profound impact we've been able to create in our small island nation of Sri Lanka.

Now I have a question I want you to consider.

What if you only had 6 months to live?

Dear reader, I extend this invitation for you to take a moment to pause, to still the restless currents of daily life, and to reflect upon this profound question about what really matters. Allow it to permeate the layers of your consciousness and evoke a sense of introspection. In this contemplative space, we're able to uncover the opportunity to reassess our priorities, to scrutinise the trajectory of our lives, and to make conscious choices that align with our deepest values.

As we engage with this degree of profound self-inquiry, we might find the answers to be as unique and diverse as the individuals who seek them. This is because each person's journey unfolds along a distinct path, guided by their values, aspirations, and experiences.

Some may choose to embark on grand adventures, exploring the farthest corners of the Earth and immersing themselves in the kaleidoscope of human cultures. Others may choose to dedicate their time to acts of service and philanthropy, finding deep fulfilment in making a positive impact on the lives of others. Meanwhile, some may prioritise the cultivation of inner peace and wisdom, seeking solace in spiritual practices and contemplation. And yet, others may find solace in the simple joys of everyday life, cherishing the precious moments with loved ones, and finding beauty in 'ordinary' things.

As you've already read, I confronted this profound question myself. My journey veered onto a transformational path that led me to forsake the trappings of a conventional career in the interest of embracing a life of purpose and service, and to embark on a quest for inner growth and resilience. It is my hope that you too, dear reader, will find the courage to navigate the depths of this inquiry to make choices that resonate with the core of your being, and to live a life filled with authenticity, meaning, and profound fulfilment.

Together, let us strive to create a world where transformative change is not a distant dream but a lived reality. It will be a world where compassion, mindfulness, and resilience are woven into the fabric of our collective existence.

CHAPTER FOUR

Unlocking Our Children's Uniqueness

Alex Blake

Alex Blake used to mine diamonds – now she is passionate about coaching clients to mine the diamonds in their hearts. Using her magical ability to unlock true potential, Alex guides you to realising your unique gifts and strengths.

Alex has managed multi-million-dollar construction projects and trekked Mount Kilimanjaro, yet she counts her greatest adventure as parenting her two boys. She is an author and international speaker and the founder of 'Diamond Stories – The Heart Centered Publisher', where she assists clients in sharing their stories in books. So, if your heart is yearning for you to live a more abundant life, or it has a narrative you need to share with the world – Alex is your woman!

You can contact Alex at
www.diamondstories.au
alex@diamondstories.au

There weren't a lot of opportunities to spend time alone with either of my parents when I was a child, but I learnt a lot from the moments when I did. Being one of six kids meant there was always something to be done or something to prepare for, whether it was getting ready for school each morning, getting to the bus stop on time, doing homework, or training for that season's sport in the afternoons: netball and soccer in winter; athletics, tennis, and swimming in summer.

I don't remember ever seeing Mum sitting still. When I woke each day for school with frost glistening on the window, my mind groggy with sleep and my toes tingling with cold, she would already be outside by the clothesline hanging the laundry. When I got home, she'd be sitting at the dining table sorting shirts and pairing socks, with a cup of half-drunk weak black tea nestled near the fraying cane basket. For the rest of the afternoon her time was consumed by driving us to training, preparing dinner, or watering her beautiful garden.

Mum's garden was a marvel of colours, shapes, and scents. Almost daily she would wander through it wearing her floppy sun hat and canvas gloves, caressing a petal here, laying fresh mulch there, frowning at the damage caused by frost or an errant slug. She moved easily, unhurried, knowing intuitively what the garden needed. Here, her entire being slowly transitioned from the busyness of being Mum and the many needs nipping at her heels, to the whole person she was. She was not 'doing' for her family; she was just 'being' for herself.

Children have an organic need to connect with their parents and on the days when I felt that need most fiercely, I'd join her in the garden. That was the only time I could be alone with her.

It was my opportunity to connect with her 'being'. Surrounded by the blossoms and stems, the heady fragrance of gardenias, the faint humming of bees and the gentle bobbing of purple lavender turrets, I would ask Mum a question or share what was worrying me.

Most of the time, her response went something like this: "It will all work out. Try not to worry."

With her answer tucked safely in my mind, I'd stand by her side in stillness. Together, we'd watch the water jet from the hose shove the wispy stems about and the droplets escape down waxy leaves. I asked lots of questions, more to hear her voice than out of any desire to increase my knowledge of plants. She may have seen it differently, but from my perspective, from the time I was seven to 17, she was connected to herself here. And in this space, this place where she was so content to just be, I felt connected to her.

So many of us are raised in societies and families where being busy and 'doing' is applauded. I would love for us to understand that 'being' is what connects us to fulfilment and joy. Being enables us to thrive.

I grew up believing that feeling my emotions deeply and expressing myself fully and frequently was usually not convenient for others. There wasn't time for the adults to pause and wait for me to finish expressing myself because there were five other children for them to take care of.

I am the third eldest child in my family. I was six years old the day my fifth sibling was born. Saying goodbye to Mum at the hospital that night left me in tears. As our car pulled into the driveway at home, one of my siblings looked at me with more disapproval than curiosity and asked, "Why are you still crying?"

Dad responded for me, sighing deeply as he explained, "Alex feels things differently to others." On reflection, I can see that those words reinforced the story I had made up and lived by when I was just a small child. That story was about the fact that feeling too much and fully expressing myself would be met with disapproval, conflict, and ultimately, rejection.

My belief in that story taught me that controlling my emotions was safe. Controlling my tears was safe. Controlling my space and being seen as holding it all together was safe. Feeling too much and sharing my feelings was not safe.

This unconscious belief was reinforced in my teens when I steered away from sharing how I felt, but patiently listened to friends telling me about their tumultuous boy dramas for hours. It was also reinforced throughout my career as an engineer where processes ruled, and emotion had no place. It turned my life inside out when I became a mother and emotion spilled out of every pore of my son's little body.

The point I want to make here is that seeing the uniqueness in our children and supporting them as they express themselves fully is integral to creating an environment where they can thrive as they grow up. Encouraging their gifts, talents, and strengths, as well as allowing them to own and express their inherent nature is the validation a child needs to live their sovereign life.

I slowly learned that the greatest gift I could give my child was to hold space for him. To allow him the safety he needed to express himself. And it was hard. I was conflicted and often depressed. Choosing to give him this space meant leaving playdates early and feeling the critical looks from other parents. It meant saying no to invitations to gatherings in homes and restaurants, even though I desperately wanted to feel less isolated through engaging in conversations with adults. Prioritising his needs meant saying no to childcare services and holiday camps, even though I longed for a break. It was too much to expect carers to hold the space for my son's little body to express frustration when he didn't have the words to articulate what he was feeling. Fortunately, playgrounds, bikes, hiking, and swimming saved us. Like in my mother's garden, these were the places we could be present.

As parents, we're responsible for holding space for our children so that they can express themselves fully. Yes, it might be messy, uncharted, and uncertain territory, but that's the space our kids need for nature to do what it is intended to do – to help them grow up.

Without us holding a safe container for them to explore, their ideas and imaginations cannot expand.

Children need both emotional space and energetic space. There is no guarantee that providing this environment won't create tension. In fact, tension (not stress) is an ideal space for creating. Tension offers excitement for the possibility of having what we desire, and when it is present, it means that something new is being created. This is important because we're responsible for allowing the full expression of our children's uniqueness to create and think and feel deeply. We're also responsible for understanding what's going on inside our own head because we will unconsciously (and sometimes consciously) make choices for our children based on our agenda rather than theirs.

When we have an agenda, it usually means that an outcome of some kind is required. That outcome is about something tangible being produced, a schedule being met, or a certificate being acquired. How different would the world be if we routinely encouraged our children to make their own choices? Children know what they want. They know when they're ready to go beyond their comfort zone and grow.

For our children to thrive, we need to guide them to live life expressing their inherent nature, and that might not completely fit into the mould created by the societal or familial traditions that surround them. The way I see it, traditions are a bit of a double-edged sword. While on the one hand they are grounding and fulfilling, they can also be stifling and limiting. That said, it is a joy to share traditions with our children, and it's our responsibility to honour our children's choices, whether they choose to lead a life that is aligned with the traditions in question or not. The bottom line is that holding space without judgement is what it takes to reinforce their feelings of belonging, significance, and love.

If what you've read so far has resonated with you, you might be wondering what you need to do to empower your children to just be themselves. My advice would be that whenever your child comes to you wanting to express something, just listen, and when they're done, say, "That's an interesting perspective. Thank you for sharing it with me." or "You have strong feelings about this. Thank you for expressing how you feel." Resist expressing negativity or criticism. Instead, let them know that it's ok if they don't feel the same way as you do, and that respecting other people's views is important.

After all, judgements come from your beliefs and how you understand the world to be. You're entitled to have your own perspective of what is right and wrong respected, just as you're responsible for respecting the perspectives of others. The thing to recognise is that if you disagree with your child's perspective, you'll actually be in the position to build your relationship with them if you have a discussion rather than an argument. You could even consider sharing why you hold a certain belief with them.

Demonstrating this kind of self-awareness is a powerfully freeing approach for both you and your child.

As an engineer in diamond mines, I got good at finding the precious gems in lumps of rock. There was a thrill in that for me. It's even more thrilling finding the jewels in a person's heart and allowing them to surface and be expressed genuinely. I created my company, Diamond Stories, to do just that.

I love visiting schools around the globe, especially in developing countries, and helping children tell their stories, both real and imagined. My goal is to share my passion and provide children with the resources needed for living out their heart's purpose. This means supplying them with things like books, writing and art supplies, musical instruments, lunch, reading rooms and teachers. Through our student scholarships, Diamond Stories Collection is supporting the sustainability of communities and the growth and uniqueness of children all over the world. My hope is to leave a legacy where children have access to everything they need to unlock their potential and exist in the highest expression of themselves.

When I walk into the classroom the children's eyes widen, and grins emerge on their little faces. "Who wants to write a story?" I ask. I love watching as their initial wariness gives way to curiosity, then delight, as they laugh and wriggle in their seats with the anticipation of letting their stories flow freely. It's probably the first time they've been encouraged to use their imagination. As they begin to understand that this time and space is for them, they might look dreamily out the window or grasp a pencil and just begin to write. As they write, a quietness lingers over us, punctuated by the gentle rustle of paper. When I ask, "Who is ready to share?" hands shoot up and the little authors' faces beam when they start sharing stories of family, friendship, dreams, and imagination. Some stories are taped to the crumbling wall and celebrated; others are shyly squeezed into my hand to read alone because nerves took centre stage that day. They are eager to share who they are, and I see myself in these beautiful children.

Holding space for children and witnessing them express their uniqueness is one of the joys of my life. I love listening to their perspectives and how they see themselves in the world. When children feel safe to express themselves, their imaginations are engaged, and they have the freedom and potential to create. That's how the diamonds in their hearts are allowed to shine.

I want to invite you to empower the children in your life to discover their own natural abilities and gifts. With your support, they are capable of 'being' who they really are.

I also love helping people tell the stories they've always wanted to tell. Through my work with Diamond Stories, I am privileged to help adults express themselves through my writing and life coaching programs. Some want to write books, others want to create a life they love, and others just want to be heard … their way.

Just as my mother was being her true self in her garden, I am expressing my highest potential when I embody my gift of unlocking the true diamonds in the things that I create. I would love for the next generation to be raised knowing that being and expressing themselves is what makes them thrive.

CHAPTER FIVE

The need for NLP in an AI World

Sonya Furlong

Sonya Furlong stands among Australia's top-tier Master Trainers in Neuro-Linguistic Programming (NLP), offering life-changing coaching and training programs. As the owner of the Centre for Life Therapies, she has created a holistic haven for mental well-being and personal growth. Sonya's commitment extends further through the Centre for Life Therapies Foundation, striving to provide underprivileged Australian communities access to the empowering NLP tools. Her overarching mission is to elevate global consciousness, and in its initial phase, she aims to empower 260,000 Australians to unlock their true potential by imparting NLP skills, with the aim to making a profound impact on our collective journey.

You can contact Sonia at
www.centreforlifetherapies.com
linkedin.com/in/sonyafurlongnlptrainer

Since the beginning of time, humans have struggled to be 'good enough' and feel 'worthy'. Today, instead of being terrified of interacting with a powerful sabre-toothed tiger, people are terrified of interacting with a powerful executive. Both situations could provide food for the family, or have dire consequences.

As I write this chapter in 2023, there are two massive tools emerging that can help us attain the lives we want. Both have been around for decades, used by relatively few people to get further faster for their families and their careers. I'm talking about Artificial Intelligence (AI) and Neuro-Linguistic Programming (NLP).

It's scary that AI will soon become 'smarter' than humans in many ways. Smarter? Really? I'm here to tell you that data and wisdom are two very different things. And while AI can crunch way more data than human brains can, true wisdom can only be cultivated by people. That's why NLP can grow your wisdom to help you move through life stronger, better, and faster.

In 2016, when I first stumbled upon NLP, it sparked a revolution in my life. I couldn't help but wonder:

"Where had this remarkable instrument of personal development been hiding all these years?"

For the first time in decades, I had a structure for mental processes, and an instruction manual for my thoughts, decisions, and actions. I was no longer struggling with mental highs and lows, confused about why life was happening 'to' me instead of 'for' me.

With the daily use of NLP processes, I can now keep my mind focused, my emotions well-managed, my decisions insightful, my goals clearly defined and achievable, and my relationships open and meaningful. My intelligence and emotions are now being continually sharpened and upgraded.

NLP allows me to dig deep into my unconscious mind to heal past traumas and align myself to my true values. It gives me a proven framework for creating an endless stream of meditations and writings to educate and inspire my clients and students at the Centre for Life Therapies, which I founded 7 years ago. NLP allows me to unpack difficult situations and find pleasing outcomes that benefit the greater good. The clear structure increases my emotional intelligence and makes it easy to teach it to others.

But there is another modern miracle that has all the headlines. AI are the two letters on everyone's lips.

Artificial Intelligence speeds up the workflow for many professionals. No wonder it is sweeping the world with new applications performing superhuman feats every day. And you should use it too. Otherwise, some whiz kid down the hall might eventually get your job. At the very least, I recommend you dabble in it. That will be enough for you to keep up and get ahead.

Unfortunately, as more people use AI for high level thinking, many are using their own intelligence less. AI can process huge amounts of information in minutes that would take a human days, or even months to process. The only problem is that this creates a real risk that people's brains will become weak from lack of use.

Neuroscience confirms that our mind is like a muscle which improves with consistent training and being challenged. At the mental gym, weight training includes critical thinking, problem-solving, learning new skills, and practicing mindfulness. These skills enhance cognitive abilities by growing new neuro connections and strengthening existing ones through a process called neuroplasticity.

What happens when we don't use our brains and rely on AI to do the thinking for us? Scientists call it 'cognitive stagnation' or 'mental stagnation'. What are the symptoms and outcomes of cognitive or mental stagnation? Let's take a look:

1. A Decline in cognitive abilities: Just as muscles atrophy when they're not used, cognitive skills can deteriorate when they're not regularly exercised. This makes it harder for people to learn new information, solve problems and tackle novel situations.

2. Reduced neuroplasticity: Neuroplasticity is the brain's ability to reorganise and form new connections. Weakening that through lack of use makes it harder for the brain to adapt to new information or tasks.

3. Memory issues: Engaging in cognitive challenges helps improve the functioning of our memory. Without such engagement, long-term and short-term memory are compromised. That affects our view of the world, which in turn affects our thoughts and behaviours.

4. Mood and mental health: Mental stagnation tends to create boredom and frustration, as well as anxiety and depression.

5. Slower information processing: Without regular cognitive engagement, the brain's efficiency and processing speed decreases.

6. Negative impact on brain structure: Studies suggest that a lack of mental stimulation could have long-term structural effects on the brain because neuronal connections may weaken or decline in number over time.

7. Difficulty paying attention: The ability to selectively focus and filter out distracting stimuli enables us to concentrate on specific tasks. Needless to say, attention plays a crucial role in processing information, as well as getting things done.

8. Executive functions diminish: Skills such as planning, problem-solving, decision-making and self-control rely on a healthy brain. This is important because executive functions help us regulate our behaviour, manage complex tasks, and achieve goals.

9. Sophisticated language and communication skills are lost: The ability to communicate with one another enables us to maintain human connection, and to convey and understand complex ideas.

10. Difficulty socialising: The ability to notice and interpret social cues, recognise emotions in others, and engage in social interactions with one another is key to our quality of life.

11. Lack of creativity: Innovative ideas and solutions decrease in people who have less diverse experiences and mental challenges. Creativity and innovation are

uniquely human capabilities that are essential for progress and success.

As AI usage increases within the home, school, and workplace, how can we ensure the ongoing vitality of our minds? Among other things, NLP trainers provide fitness for our cognitive faculties.

Understanding Neuro-Linguistic Programming

NLP which was developed in the 1970s by Professor John Grinder and Richard Bandler is a multidisciplinary approach to understanding human communication, behaviour, and subjective experience. It provides techniques and methodologies for identifying and modifying the patterns of thought and behaviour that affect our potential. It draws upon elements from psychology, linguistics, and neurology to unlock new ways of achieving personal growth.

The Crucial Role of NLP in the Age of AI

Just as the gym supports physical strength, NLP builds cognitive strength. Just like a personal trainer at the gym, an NLP trainer offers a diverse range of mental workouts that stimulate critical thinking, problem-solving, and communication skills. This helps unlock our potential for analysis, behaviour modelling and emotional intelligence for better relationships and a more rewarding career.

What I love about NLP is that it enhances active thinking by providing individuals with the tools to think critically, explore new perspectives, and adapt to changing circumstances.

These abilities are indispensable in a world of AI-driven transformations.

NLP Processes to Develop Emotional Intelligence

Emotional intelligence is the ability to understand and manage emotions. It distinguishes humans from machines. NLP techniques facilitate the development of emotional intelligence by improving self-awareness, empathy, and communication skills. These capabilities are essential for building meaningful relationships, collaborating effectively, and leading with empathy.

Here are three techniques from the NLP playbook that help develop our brain and our emotional intelligence:

1. Active listening and reflective communication: Engaging in active listening involves not just hearing the words spoken by others, but also understanding the underlying emotions, context, and nonverbal cues. By practicing reflective communication, where you paraphrase and summarize what you've heard, you'll exercise your brain's language processing centres and enhance your ability to empathize with others. This process nurtures emotional intelligence by fostering better understanding and connection, while also sharpening your cognitive skills so that you can process more complex verbal information.

2. Positive self-talk and affirmations: This involves consciously controlling your self-talk and reframing negative thoughts into positive affirmations. By doing that you can reshape your cognitive patterns and

emotional responses. This practice not only cultivates a more optimistic mindset, but also rewires your brain's neural pathways, promoting resilience and self-awareness which are both key components of emotional intelligence.

3. Mindfulness and visualisation: Engaging in mindfulness meditation and guided visualization exercises are integral parts of neuro-linguistic programming. These processes encourage you to focus your attention on the present moment, observe your thoughts without judgment, and vividly imagine positive outcomes. Regular mindfulness practice supports brain plasticity by strengthening the prefrontal cortex and enhancing emotional regulation. It also heightens emotional intelligence by promoting self-awareness, reducing stress reactivity, and bolstering your capacity to manage emotions effectively.

The Best of Both Miracles

If you want to compete in the modern age with less stress and more ability, it is best if you learn both of these miraculous tools. NLP will help shed your baggage, build your personal and business relationships, and give you the clarity to map out the most enjoyable, practical, and profitable road to follow. Then when you put some AI in your fuel tank, your wheels will turn faster than your competition. You'll be halfway to your destination while they're still crunching numbers like cavemen with hammers and rocks.

Fortunately, NLP and AI are both way easier to learn than you think. I suggest you start dabbling in both. Watch a YouTube video here and there, read some blogs, or sign up for short courses in both AI and NLP.

Of course, as you start to feel how much stronger, smarter and faster NLP can make you, then you will want to learn more and grow more. You will find your life being easier, more fun, and more meaningful. You will have more options, and more opportunities for your career and your family.

AI will help tremendously, but without getting NLP training, you'll risk bringing your baggage with you. The same tendency toward self-sabotage; short circuiting of your relationships; having clouded vision; wondering what on earth is going on with people in your life; and feeling like the world is leaving you behind, may continue at an exponential rate as AI becomes common place.

NLP can transform your life just like it did mine. That's why my mission is to make it as common as any other training. It's literally the manual for your mind. No wonder people go out of their mind; it's a mess in there unless you learn how to clean it up. Then it's smooth sailing with your head in the game and enjoying it.

As AI permeates every socioeconomic culture, there is no shortage of visibility there. On the other hand, NLP is not as well known. Sure, presidents like Barack Obama, famous filmmakers like the Wachowski sisters, and many successful executives and leaders know about it, that's why they're on top. But why stop there? My personal mission is to bring it to the

THE NEED FOR NLP IN AN AI WORLD

rest of the world by uplifting the consciousness of the planet by 1%, using NLP. For me, this is a matter of global importance.

Conclusion

While AI helps people work faster, NLP helps us become innately smarter. And as AI does more of our thinking for us, it is crucial that we preserve and enhance our human cognitive abilities. NLP offers a powerful approach to keeping our brains active, adaptive, and empowered. By teaching specific processes for critical thinking, creativity, emotional intelligence, and personal growth, NLP equips people with the skills necessary to navigate the challenges and opportunities presented by AI. NLP is becoming more essential to harness the full potential of our minds and ensure a prosperous future.

I believe the rise of AI necessitates the rise of NLP. Just as AI reduces the need for us to think for ourselves, NLP increases our ability to think holistically about ourselves and others. AI cultivates data. NLP cultivates wisdom. AI literally helps machines learn and grow. NLP helps our soul learn and grow. And as you read that now, I'm willing to bet your soul is feeling the need to grow faster than machines do. But it's not a competition; you can enjoy building clarity and wisdom through NLP, so that when you use AI to move quickly you will know you're going in the right direction.

AI without NLP is a bit like a toddler playing with a hammer. AI with some NLP training is like that toddler growing up to be Leonardo Da Vinci, working on a masterpiece. Now is the greatest time in all of history to make a masterpiece of your

ONYA FURLONG

life with these amazing new tools. I hope you will join me in bringing this to the world.

64

CHAPTER SIX

Mental Health is a Matter of Global Importance

Kerry Howard

Kerry Howard is a best-selling author and former psychologist, now in-demand workplace mental health consultant. Kerry is a maverick in the field of mental health. She has won multiple national and international awards for her innovation in wellbeing, including two international awards for her commitment to treating PTSD and improving mental health in Australia. In 2021 Kerry won the Excellence in Science and Technology Award for her pioneering work in the delivery of online trauma therapy. Kerry's new book 'How to Heal a Workplace: tackle trauma, promote psychological safety' *and boost happiness at work* was launched in February 2023 and provides insights into how traumatic experiences in the workplace can result in psychosocial injuries. In this book she interviews senior leaders and affected workers across industry sectors and provides innovation in workplace wellbeing to prevent injuries. How to Heal a Workplace has been nominated in the 2023 Australian Business Book Awards.

You can contact Kerry at
www.kerryannhoward.com
linkedin.com/in/chief-mental-health-advisor

When we consider how many things have changed in our post-pandemic world, it is positive to see that awareness around mental health is at the highest level in our recorded history. Considering the negative legacy of the pandemic, the fact that we have greater awareness and acceptance of the connection between our mental health and physical health being strongly tied together is a significant positive change in the status quo. Finally, we have recognised mental health as equally important to physical health in the overall management of our wellbeing.

Community awareness has grown exponentially over a very short period of time, but with it has grown significant anxiety about how we are supposed to manage these challenges with some level of balance. The problem is that if we cater to all potential mental health challenges that individuals experience by supporting inaction in the face of them, we enable blockers that prevent us working through these challenges. In this way, we prevent the individual engaging in personal growth through empowerment. Rather, we inadvertently reinforce the mindset that we can't take action in the face of the emotional reaction or negative feelings that we may experience.

This is an essential element we need to understand about our modern world and our response to it. Acknowledging and validating our emotions is important, however we often enable the feeling that the emotion evokes to stop us taking any action. The problem with this is that inactivity in response to the feeling will reinforce a victim state and stifle any opportunity for the individual to develop resilience.

The phenomenon of resistance to change is not uncommon in our human experience. A degree of resistance is a normal precursor to the process of adjusting our thinking to any area of our life that needs to change. In order for our approach to be adjusted we need to overcompensate to shift our thinking. In psychological terms, we call this an Attribution Bias. It is essentially the process that we need to take to significantly alter our thinking. When we have already judged something as negative, we need to start telling everyone how incredibly positive it is in order to justify our own shift in attitude.

Let me give you a quick example. Have you ever found that you met someone for the first time, and for some reason you didn't like them? After a while, you may get to know them better, or they do something positive that caused you to feel like you must have been wrong about them. What's more, you then found yourself speaking more positively about them and extolling their good deeds to others. In essence, you wound up liking this person more than you would have if you had not made the quick decision to not like them in the first place. Why? Because in order to overcome the negative feelings we need to become twice as positive in order to change the way we feel.

At this point in human history, we are having to do this regarding mental health. What we used to downplay as 'nothing of importance' has enabled our community to ignore the veritable pandemic of mental challenges that were always there. Yet, this awareness has also brought about a significantly higher level of debilitating support. It is an unintended consequence of raising awareness that the resulting support can sometimes be too much. Mental health awareness is now so widespread and well known that it has developed a level of normality that is aiding a level of debilitation.

While it is great that we are having more open conversations around mental health and greater recognition that it is a very 'normal' part of being human, something is missing. What is missing from the conversation about mental health in our post-pandemic world is the resilience building capabilities that need to be developed, and the process of owning and working through our mental challenges. Time and again, I have seen this opportunity being missed in the case of parents with kids who are struggling, and now more than ever, it is also happening in the workplace. It is like we are too scared to provide supportive encouragement to a staff member with a mental health condition for fear that it will be labelled as harassment.

I don't believe we can tip-toe around this situation anymore. The reality is that we are looking down the barrel of a MAJOR health crisis in the community. The good news is that we can do something to turn it around. I want to be sure to provide some guidance about what I am proposing, so I will outline one of the most common mental health challenges here.

Anxiety

Anxiety is something that is commonly referred to as the reason people can't perform certain tasks or engage in particular activities. Anxiety is at its basic form a fear of the future. Anxiety is a very real mental health challenge, not a label that should be used to define someone as an 'anxious person'. They are a person who experiences anxiety in the face of certain challenges, and we need to recognise it and help the person by providing tools to support them towards a solution.

The biggest challenge we are facing in society around mental health is that as our awareness has grown around mental health conditions, so too has our fear of them. When a person says that an activity is making them anxious, the latest approach in the workplace (and many homes) is to absolve them of responsibility for having to complete the activity. Unfortunately, this approach tends to reinforce the sense of learned helplessness and robs them of an opportunity to move through their fear with support and complete the activity (even if imperfectly), which would be a much more empowering experience for the individual.

It's not hard to see why absolving someone of a responsibility that is making them feel anxious might appear to be empathic, however we are essentially stripping them of an opportunity to develop resilience in the face of their anxiety.

We have seen this in many societies as a reaction to the pandemic. In general, anxiety disorders are affecting many more members of our community than we have ever seen before. This is particularly the case because the fear response is triggered by something that cannot be seen or felt, therefore our fear of it has to be imbibed in trust and belief. In essence, we had to create the fear to get people to take action through conditioning, to embrace social distancing and consider inoculation. In our post-pandemic world, as the threat has reduced, we now need to extinguish the fear that has developed to enable people to get on with living.

You may have heard of the Pavlov's Dog experiments where the psychological researcher Pavlov trained dogs to salivate to the sound of a ringing bell. He did this first by 'pairing' the experience of the sound of the bell being closely followed by food, gradually delaying the food being offered until the dog would drool when the bell was rung in total absence of food. Once this pairing was created and the dog would routinely salivate to the sound of a bell, then Pavlov proceeded to extinguish the conditioning by ringing the bell and not ever offering food. This experiment was considered ground-breaking because it showed that the dogs required twice as much time to extinguish the conditioning than they did to create it.

If we apply the same notion to the way humans responded to the pandemic, it's interesting to note that it has taken three years to get back to some level of 'normal' functioning in our society. We still see individuals and governments highlighting concerns regarding Covid-19, and some people are still taking strong preventative actions, but for the most part, we are now travelling and interacting as we were before the pandemic. However, the longer-term implications are that it will take more like six years to really return to the way things were in 2019, and that is only if we don't have any other similar health issues to contend with during this time.

So, how do we use this enhanced awareness to improve our insights into our own mental health without allowing it to debilitate us? A good place to start would be to normalise the fact that sometimes we are not doing so well, without making us need to label it as something abnormal. In short, it's about choosing awareness, adding some compassion into the mix, and consciously building resilience.

Whilst we didn't choose to be conditioned, we can consciously choose to extinguish any conditioning that isn't serving us.

Recovery not Dependency

Personally, I believe the pandemic normalised mental health and raised it to its rightful place as a contributor to our overall sense of wellbeing. This is important because in the past it was always approached from the perspective of fear of the unknown, with words like 'crazy' or 'insane' used to describe distressed humans. Whereas now, we have much greater insight into our emotional reactions and responses. This is key because it is the acceptance of the fact that life is not always going to be easy, and there could be times when we just want to pull the bed quilt over our head and shut the world out, that makes it okay – normal, in fact! This is a temporary response to a feeling, and it helps to keep everything in perspective. What's more, being able to be honest with yourself, and open with others is empowering.

I really love the fact that being open to the full range of human emotional states and their varying expressions is being normalised in our community. In essence, we have extinguished the notion that anxiety and depression are unusual – rather we have become aware that we can experience fear of the future (anxiety) and shame of our past (depression) at varying times in our lives depending on what is going on around us, and still be a resourceful contributor to humanity. In normalising these emotional reactions, we can also recognise how common they really are. This is important because when we adopt such a perspective, we can learn to help ourselves.

The challenge for all of us is to learn to develop greater awareness of our emotional fluctuations and then understand how we can improve our own mental health. In my book 'The Trouble With Trauma', I outline how you can learn about your 'Self-Management System', that I call our SMS. Awareness of this system enables people to not only understand themselves, but also recognise their own emotional reactivity to a variety of situations in life. In my latest book, 'How to Heal a Workplace', I outline how to apply the SMS to individual members of teams in the context of helping them to recognise their own emotional triggers that have the potential to show up in the workplace.

In essence, the key to recovery is to develop greater self-awareness and insight. Once we have that, it makes it much easier to recognise our own reactions and enable us to make considered responses.

Technological Solutions

As humanity moves towards greater self-awareness, an opportunity will arise for us to utilise Artificial Intelligence enabled systems to provide high quality and consistent psychoeducation at a minimal cost. I imagine some of you may be thinking that mental health is not an appropriate use case for AI because, after all, humans are such complex creatures that we feel that we need to be understood by an extremely well trained and compassionate human therapist. However, where AI really steps into the limelight is in its ability to be consistent and non-judgemental – unlike a human therapist.

From my perspective as an empowerment therapist, I see this as the perfect opportunity for resolving mental health challenges as it enables people to take their power back and recover.

How will these technological advancements affect our mental health? When we experience rapid change in our environment, we can really struggle to adapt to those changes unless we can see benefit in them. The truth is that the adoption of AI is already prolific. In fact, there are very few people who don't interact with some level of AI in their day to day lives. From using Alexa or Siri, to asking about the weather or directions, to calling government departments on the telephone, AI is being utilised in many and varied ways throughout our society.

This doesn't mean that everyone is going to like developments in the use of AI when it comes to mental health. However, these advancements have progressed too far to be stopped. Whether we like it or not, we are going to have to learn to adapt to them. It is situations like this that reinforce the fact that it is our reaction to the experiences we encounter in life that determines the quality of life we enjoy. In other words, now that you are aware of the way conditioning can result in a sense of inevitability about the way life is, you can make a real difference to how your life plays out by taking an active role in managing the emotional responses you have to the things that happen on a day-to-day basis. This is why the development of greater self-awareness is so important, as is the ability to cope with regular and rapid change.

The Future Is Now

It is fair to say that prior to the pandemic we had no clear insight into the many and varied use cases for AI adoption, cryptocurrencies, or Web3, let alone the fourth dimension and beyond. As with all of the transition points in human history that have resulted in significant changes to the way we live, the key to surviving is the ability that we all have to adapt quickly and anticipate the next shift in human thinking.

As we experience things, they change, just as our experiences change us through the paradigms we create. As we create these paradigms, we have the power to shift them. In fact, our ability to develop incredible self-awareness provides the perfect environment for paradigm shifts to happen. This is an important point because as humans we need to become comfortable with the constantly changing landscape of our outer world, and develop an internal strength that ensures this doesn't negatively affect our inner world. It's about making sure our fear of change doesn't hinder our ability to not only survive, but to actually thrive.

We need to do this by educating ourselves better, and recognising that the ability to heal is within us, and that the feeling of being a victim is brought about by externalising the solution to our humanness onto another person to correct.

We all need to develop a conscientious spirit that is very self-aware and not only supportive of others, but compassionate toward ourselves as well. Living a fulfilled life isn't about knowing everything, it's about knowing where to go to find the information we need to resolve any problems we encounter. In this way we develop insight into our human experience, and a true level of mind and body connection that will enable us all to resolve any emotional or physical challenges that might come our way.

Self-aware, self-sufficient and self-fulfilling. These are the humans who will be equipped to resolve their own mental health challenges into the future.

CHAPTER SEVEN

The Power of Self-Care

Vicky Jamieson

With more than 30 years in the wellness and anti-ageing industry, **Vicky Jamieson** has never lost her passion for sharing her wisdom to help women feel vibrant and energised to live a full life. She has been featured in wellbeing magazines, interviewed on HealthRadio in New York, and speaks on specialist skin nutrition, lifestyle strategies to avoid burnout, and support strategies to guide women through a healthy transition into Menopause. A results orientated wellness mentor and anti-ageing expert, Vicky's continual adoption of innovative solutions, integrated with traditional methods help her clients have more energy in the boardroom, at the executive table, and for their families. This has been instrumental in giving the women she works with that energy edge that sets them apart from others. Vicky has a busy Melbourne practice, offering specialised self-care treatments and nutritional education to help women harness their physical, mental and emotional growth and creativity at a time that can feel uncertain.

You can contact Vicky at
www.betterbody.net.au
linkedin.com/in/vicky-jamieson-betterbody

I used to be one of those powerhouse kinda women who prided herself on making things happen no matter what. Now that I've seen the light (so to speak), and got my own life back on track, I'm passionate about helping others to take their power to be well back into their own hands. For me, this is a matter of global importance.

One of the things that worries me is the damage I see people doing to the quality of their life through a lack of awareness about the simple steps they could be taking to set themselves up for a much more vibrant and healthful future. I'm figuring if you're still reading, I might have hit on something here that resonates with you.

I could rattle off my qualifications and share case study after case study where I've helped people to set themselves up for a much more fulfilling life, but what I'm going to do instead is assure you that I know what it's like to feel burnout tapping on the door and worrying about things getting worse as time goes on.

What got me to where I am now

A pivotal time in my life was when I was in my early forties and had a lot to be grateful for. We had recently built our dream home, I had a successful salon, two beautiful kids and a husband I loved deeply, but I felt that surely there must be more to life than this. I felt like I was stuck in Groundhog Day. My friends told me that I was just tired because of my habit of doing too much. "You're 40 now. You have to slow down" they would say.

Well, I didn't buy it. I wasn't even halfway through my life. And what's more, I sure didn't want to spend the next 20 years being bone tired and the following 20 years even more tired and achy as well. What I wanted instead was to be able to travel and play with grandkids without being fragile. I was sure there must be a better way and I was determined to prove everyone wrong!

That was the tipping point for me. I didn't realise it at the time, but there were two things at play that were making life harder for me than it should have been. Those things were stress and hormones. What I didn't know was that I was starting my journey into perimenopause. This was a term I didn't even know existed at the time. What made things worse was that I was a holistic practitioner, helping women with stress, gut health, skin health, and hormone balancing. How could I not know I was going through the start of the menopause process when I was only 42? The fact is many women don't realise they're in that position.

Luckily for me, I attended a postgraduate class on stress that provided me with the key to getting out from under the exhaustion I had been feeling. I took the quiz that was included in the course with the intention of getting through this part of the session with flying colours. Wow – I was so wrong. Out of around 80 quick fire Yes/No questions – I had scored a whopping 68 where 80 was totally stressed out. I was astounded. How could this be? What I now know is that many women at this age start to experience stress differently because of changing hormone levels. This can severely impact how we show up in the world and also create that ripple effect that people like us want to make in the world.

The great news is that I'm going to tell you how to shortcut this phase and instead live a life filled with vibrant energy, purpose and fulfilment. Whether you're the CEO of a company, a small business owner or head up an executive team of a multi-million-dollar company, the rules are the same.

I've written this chapter to empower you to set up and end your day with effective self-care rituals that will truly fill your tank and enable you to experience the vibrant energy you deserve. You could even become a human version of a lighthouse, attracting your children, peers, and other leaders to mirror your behaviour, and in so doing generationally change the way the world deals with stress.

My aim in this chapter is to make you aware of the importance of self-care and fill you in on easy ways to incorporate it into the way you go about your day, including how to effectively manage stress. I'm going to focus on stress first because it disables us in two particularly damaging ways. One of those is that it speeds up cognitive decline, and the other one is that it makes us feel more tired than we actually are because of the weight of the mental stress it imposes on us.

Getting a handle on stress starts with getting really good at recognising it. This is important because it's the way stress has become normalised that has made it into the silent killer that it actually is. But awareness is power, and once you get awareness around what your triggers for stress are, you can counteract them by doing some really simple things like patting a dog, going for a walk, having a bath, listening to some uplifting music, or doing some gentle stretching. Basically, anything that will disrupt the pattern you've possibly been playing out for years and replacing it with the body's feel-good hormones will do the trick. By doing this you will literally be rewiring your brain and changing the trajectory of your life in the process.

Managing stress is not an either/or proposition. I say that because the suggestions I've made about generating the feel-good chemicals in our brain is an antidote to stress. The other approach that is equally effective is about calming our body down.

Belly or abdominal breathing has been shown to quickly (in most cases within 3 seconds) take our body out of the so called 'fight or flight' response that is triggered when we are stressed. It's important to be able to retrain ourselves to the point where our body and mind are able to be optimised. This is why establishing a ritual of meditation or breathing is so worthwhile.

Can you imagine what it will be like when you're able to fall asleep deeply and process everything that's gone on during the day, and being able to recall the kinds of things that you find yourself unable to remember because of the poor quality of sleep you're currently getting in particular, and the continually stressed-out state of your body more generally? Not to mention waking up feeling totally refreshed every morning.

Yes, it can happen!

To that end I want to challenge you to do 30 days straight of taking 6 deep breaths at night straight after you've put your head on the pillow and notice the extent to which your stress levels decrease, and your energy levels rise.

What I'm going to do now is share the other things that I do myself, and that I coach the people I work with to do so that we are able to get up and feel alive every day.

For me, having a cup of hot water and lemon when I get up is non-negotiable. It's great for gut health, and in my own case, it's particularly helpful from the point of view of keeping me regular. I need that extra bit of help because I have IBS. The other thing that I consider to be non-negotiable is eating in a way that fuels our body so that we have sustained energy and vitality throughout the day. To that end I suggest you choose healthy protein with breakfast in particular, and maintain a generally well-balanced diet without being obsessive about it.

When it comes to the work you do, I want you to reflect on whether you are making good decisions in relation to the way you use your time in general, and the boundaries you set in particular. I know this isn't always easy, so I suggest you seek advice from mentors if this is a challenge for you.

It's also important to allow yourself some tech free periods throughout the day. It's too easy to let screens run our lives. I don't know about you, but I don't feel like that's ok. That's why I'd urge you to take control back (if you feel like you've lost it that is), and maybe set your email up with an automatic reply going out to people who send you a message telling them that you only look at emails once a day. This is just the thin end of the wedge, but I think you get the point I'm trying to make here.

Using essential oils is another thing I love doing to keep myself well. It can be an effective tool we can use to change our mood if we need to. The thing is that smell impacts the brain within 4 seconds and works directly on the limbic system that is in charge of our memory, emotions and the stress response.

As far as I'm concerned, being well generally and thriving after 40 in particular involves focusing on the way we treat ourselves on both the physical and emotional fronts. So we're going to look at each of these in turn now.

Physically

It might seem like talking about electrical and magnetic emissions is a strange place to start because surely diet and exercise are the most important aspects of keeping our body well. What I'd say to that is that I'm starting here because unlike the case with having a poor diet and failing to do any exercise, most people aren't aware of the dangers of living near overhead powerlines. This is dangerous because there are electromagnetic fields being generated by the power lines that are creating 'stress' on our body. The good news is that this can be buffered by having EMF protectors in our house.

In fact, it's a good idea to get these EMF protectors even if your house isn't close to powerlines, because it's also worth positioning them near your computer. I say this because although computers are nowhere near as damaging as living under overhead wires, there are a number of studies that outline the damage to the brain the radiation from these devices could result in over time. You might also want to consider getting blue blocker glasses to reduce the blue light emissions we get from our computer screens and tablets that undermine the production of melatonin. This is a problem because it has the knock-on effect of undermining our ability to sleep.

Also, I recommend checking the additives in your food, and avoiding the PCBs in plastic bottles and containers. I also want you to be mindful of the parabens in skincare and personal care items, as well as detergents, and the like. The problem is that the dangerous parabens within these things are absorbed through the skin. In fact, it only takes 26 seconds for chemicals to travel through the skin barrier and enter the blood stream where they have a negative impact on our endocrine system which is responsible for our hormones.

If you find yourself constantly having a sore tummy, or experiencing bloating, indigestion or heartburn, your gut microbiome (or bacteria) could be out of whack. If you're a woman going through the phase prior to menopause, your gut could be reacting to the decrease in oestrogen in your body. On the other hand, it could be a result of the increase in the toxic load your body has been having to deal with over time that is making you more susceptible to tummy irritations and inflammation.

Of course, it's important to be mindful of the nutrients we are getting from the food we eat. In fact, I want you to start thinking of food as fuel. It's simple really, because the cleaner and more wholesome the foods we eat are, the better we will be, and the less likely we are to crave sugar and sweets. The sad fact of the way we live today is that it's all but impossible to get all 56 nutrients we need on a daily basis for our body to work at its best from the food we're readily able to access. So I recommend you choose wisely from the plethora of supplements out there. I suggest that because the last thing you want to be inadvertently doing is contributing to the toxic load your body has to process on a day-to-day basis.

Now we're going to look at the importance of moving our body every day. This is especially important for the women I work with who are over 40 and are realising the same exercises they've been doing for years are not creating the same results for them anymore. The thing is that our body starts to thicken around the waist as our hormones start changing. This is a good time to start changing up our exercise and movement routines. In fact, new research specific to women shows that short high intensity workouts using heavy weights, or resistance training are the best options for burning fat and keeping stubborn belly fat from piling on. This is the dangerous visceral fat around our organs that can lead to health conditions like fatty liver, metabolic syndrome and diabetes.

Basically, what we should be doing to keep our bodies fit is a combination of cardio workouts where our heart rate is lifted, and we're finding it hard to talk while we're exercising. The kinds of activities that create these results should be scheduled in so that we're putting our body under this 'good' form of stress between 3 and 4 times per week. If we combine this with strength or resistance training 3 times a week, as well as some form of stretching or lengthening movements for our muscles, cartilage, and fascia, we will be on the right track to keeping our body physically resilient and strong.

Emotionally

I originally had what you're about to read sitting in the previous paragraph where I was talking about eating. On reflection though I decided it fits better here because it is about the ability to fill ourselves up emotionally at the same time as we're filling ourselves up with nutrients through the food we eat. One way to do that is by aiming to have a minimum of one meal per week with friends or family members in a social setting that celebrates connection and generates those feel-good hormones we touched on earlier.

It is also well known that journaling has a profound impact on emotional wellbeing as well as emotional intelligence, yet for some reason most people tend to resist doing it. Not me though. I love journaling because it feels like having a counsellor in a notebook that I can refer to whenever I like.

The way we set up the places we work, sleep, and live in is also very important when it comes to our wellbeing. I have no qualifications whatsoever in interior design, but what I do know is that removing clutter and adding things that we love into the spaces we spend time in will make the world of difference to the way we feel. Even if all you wind up doing is eliminating clutter, you will be much better off. I say that because the more clutter there is, the more likely you are to feel overwhelmed. This is bad enough, but it's even worse if it results in things like procrastination and negative self-talk.

You may have heard it said that how you do one thing is how you do everything. I believe this to be true. So it's really worth making time and space to plan out your day, and clean up the spaces you spend time in, as well as spending less time in the company of people who drain your energy.

I also recommend you establish some kind of meditation practice. It doesn't have to be fancy or extreme. It's about regularly being able to connect with whatever you believe is for your highest good and the good of the world.

Quite often I find that as they reach their mid to late 40s (and certainly around the age of 50), women start to question what life is all about. I often hear my clients say, "Surely there is more to life – what's my bigger purpose?" What I recommend is spending some quality time on the BE (from the saying "Be, Do, Have"). When you do that, you'll get clarity around the question of what to focus on (the DO), and then you'll be able to achieve the things that mean the most to you. That's way more fulfilling and productive than running around like a mad thing from one day to the next. Remember we are human beings not human doings.

The bottom line is that prioritising your own needs and setting boundaries is the ultimate gift you can give to yourself. What's more, because of the state we're able to turn up in on a day-to-day basis when self-care is the norm, it's also a gift to the other people in our life. Ultimately, I hope this chapter has helped you to see that there is a lot you can do to feel good about yourself and your future.

CHAPTER EIGHT

The Path to Fearless Leadership

Margaret MacDonald

Margaret MacDonald has a deep commitment to empowering leaders and difference makers with qualities which enable them to embrace the challenges facing humanity. She has an unwavering belief that each of us are leaders of our lives and work; we have unrealised potential and collectively are powerful beyond measure. Her profound wish is for leaders to experience joy and meaning as they strengthen their self-leadership.

Her goal is to share what she has learned through personal and professional experience as a national leader across sectors, consultancy work, and recently life and leadership coaching and mentoring.

You can contact Margaret at
macdonaldwells@gmail.com
linkedin.com/in/margmacdonaldleaderlift

I've been considering running a retreat for women with the view to helping them find their True North for a while now. By 'True North', I'm referring to their unique calling. The idea of a retreat has been motivated by the stark reality of so few people possessing the kind of self-understanding and connection with their purpose that gives direction and meaning to life.

In a beautiful example of how one thing leads to another, these musings prompted me to reflect on my own life and why I'm so passionate about helping others find their way back to themselves.

Many of us share a sense of anxiety and urgency due to the problems created by modern life because we know unless each of us wholeheartedly works towards changing the trajectory we're on, our existence on Earth is seriously threatened. The consequences of the worst-case scenario are unimaginable. That's why it's not uncommon for people to feel as if they're frozen by a sense of powerlessness. However, I believe we can be powerful beyond measure if we tap into our purpose to collectively achieve the kind of course correction the lives of the generations coming behind us literally depend on.

I can say this with confidence as I've benefited from my life and work experiences where I've been dealing with a plethora of challenges ranging from those on a national scale to those impacting teams and individuals.

Growing up, I became aware of existential challenges that seemed insurmountable for ordinary individuals, yet in adult life, I've encountered remarkable leaders who were committed to addressing the challenges we face, and in so doing, making a significant positive impact. These leaders transformed national and international decision-making and possessed the wisdom, values, and skills to alter the course of history. What these leaders had in common was the desire to create a better world. They were prepared to question existing paradigms, look at possibilities, shift dominant thinking, and harness collective effort. Through working with these people, I've learned how even small endeavours initiated by individuals can create results that surpass our expectations.

Recent research in neuroscience and psychology has revealed novel ways of thinking and acting that enable us to cut through the noise. When we are freed from the negative energy emanating from both our internal dialogue and external media, it's easier to see that we have the potential to achieve far more than we believe. I say that because by focusing on our True North and learning how to lead from within, we initiate paradigm shifts and adopt empowered approaches to life through new ways of perceiving the world and our place within it. This opens the door to a deeper level of self-awareness which expands our personal agency because we perceive life differently. When that's the case, we can choose to reprogram our thinking, shift our focus, and embrace possibilities with optimism, courage, and resilience.

Dr. Clare Graves's bio-psychosocial research demonstrates that there is no known limit to what we can achieve. It shines the light on the thinking and value systems we must cultivate individually and societally to grow our ability to face the problems that have the potential to elude our understanding.

The increasing shift of focus to humanity and sustainability that I'm noticing picking up speed, is amplified by the alignment of our purpose and values. This powerful synergy of forces creates almost ideal conditions for building a new way of being in the world. I say that because our ability to express the qualities we need for effective leadership is generated from within. That's why my approach to leadership incorporates whole brain thinking and the integration of cognitive, emotional, and social intelligence. This is important because we need all of these capacities in our quest to live a life of meaning and purpose. What's more, when we're working from a space of collective energy our results can be harnessed to reap positive effects for the world.

In this chapter I humbly share insights drawn from personal experiences that inadvertently led me on a quest to deepen my capacity for living a joyful and meaningful life while consciously seeking ways to contribute to a more compassionate and sustainable world. These experiences have significantly influenced my thoughts, shaped my values, and fuelled my mission to effect positive change wherever possible. I'm sharing this information about myself and my background with you here because I know that whatever I have within me that helped me to traverse adversity and come out the other side even stronger is also within you.

Now that you know where I am coming from, what I want to do is provide a glimpse into some of the significant moments and influences that have shaped me.

A Conversation That Fundamentally Shaped My Perspective

I vividly recall a conversation with my father when I was just five years old. I sought solitude in the backyard because I was upset about a disappointing school report. When he came across me in that state he said, "This is only the first report. You are a clever girl, and you can achieve whatever you want. It's your choice." In that moment, my father challenged my self-perception and instilled an understanding that rather than the things that happen to me, it's the choices I make that shape my life. This early lesson in developing personal agency and the power of self-belief became the foundation for my True North orientation.

The Drive for Equality and Environmental Consciousness

I became acutely aware of gender inequality and the limitations placed on women while growing up in a rural farming community. Observing the disparities between my brothers' opportunities and those available to the females in the community ignited a visceral desire for equality within me. At the same time, my concern for the environment was sparked by witnessing unnecessary and destructive land clearing practices as well as the environmental consequences of overfishing. These formative experiences kindled feminist instincts and fuelled my passion for sustainability. This focus that was strengthened through layers of experience shaped my purpose and continues to propel me to advocate for equality and work towards a more ecologically conscious world. It actually became an integral focus of my personal and professional life.

Questioning Conventions and Cultivating Curiosity

From my early years, I often questioned the status quo and pondered the reasons for social discord and stubborn resistance to change. I couldn't help but wonder why people fixated on differences instead of seeing the benefits of working together. This early curiosity birthed a lifelong habit of questioning and an ongoing drive to understand human behaviour. While frequently receiving dismissive responses from those around me, I continued to persevere in spite of challenging prevailing norms. Unbeknownst to me, these experiences were not only shaping my values, thought processes and decision-making, but they were also paving the way for my journey into self-leadership.

Unboxing Beliefs and Overcoming Self-Sabotage

I experienced pervasive self-doubt and fear of judgment from an early age. It wasn't until my late twenties when I undertook the Myers-Briggs Type Indicator assessment that I gained life-changing insights into my approach to life. Among other things, I discovered that I had an 'uncommon type'. That awareness not only explained my nagging sense of being unacceptably different, but it also revealed my unique strengths and tendencies, such as strong intuition, a future orientation, and the ability to see patterns and translate abstract ideas into practice.

Thinking about it now, I still recall the long-term emotional impact of believing something was inherently wrong with me because of my 'deficits'. What I mean by deficits is that I struggle with details. This meant that following instructions and having an orderly approach to tasks proved a constant challenge before I realised that I had something valuable to contribute. Once I realised that, instead of trying to 'fix myself', I allowed myself to lean into my strengths and devise strategies to compensate for my less-developed traits. I also got to see the value of differences in my thinking and decision-making patterns, and I gained insight into how I could harness the power of bringing different perspectives and skills into my life and work.

These realisations changed my life in a myriad of ways. Among other things, I became more respectful of others' strengths, and I was able to interpret situations in a more nuanced way. It was nothing short of a blessing to be able to understand the motivations of others better. What's more, as I developed a heightened level of self-compassion and self-trust, I became more aware of the needs of others in particular, and relationship dynamics in general. Another key benefit of understanding myself better was that I was able to tame what I now know to be self-sabotaging thoughts that (despite having a history of high performance) resulted in more or less crippling self-diminishment, anxiety, self-isolation and feeling like I was a fraud.

Aligning with My True North and Embracing Personal Change

Clarifying my purpose was a process that took time and effort. It meant crystallising what I deeply care about and will stand up for if I need to. It transcends the roles I fulfil and the work I am engaged in. It represents my overarching aspirations for my time in the world and underpins what gives my life meaning. In effect, purpose serves as my North Star guiding my path while enduring core values act as the touchstone for decision-making in both leadership and life. The way it works for me is that my purpose shapes my goals, and the values I hold like integrity, courage, and persistence continually evolve to align with my personal growth and life circumstances.

Life disruptions have the effect of causing us to question our identity, our perception of success, our purpose, values, career choices, and relationships. During one of these transformative phases, I embarked on coaching training initially to enhance my communication skills and amplify my influence. Little did I anticipate that my journey into the intricate realm of human behaviour would be the catalyst for the emergence of genuine self-leadership. This deep period of self-exploration proved to be a profoundly challenging, humbling, and liberating experience, as it exposed stark disparities between my self-perceived identity and the reality of how I manifested myself in the world. By unveiling the hidden drivers, beliefs, imperfections, and blind spots within me, I underwent a transformative shift in my mindset that enabled me to understand the need to live my life much more consciously.

Crucially, this deep interruption led me to a pivotal realisation. That realisation was that our ability to influence others depends on the qualities we cultivate within ourselves, and our capacity to enact change begins with self-transformation. The extent to which we can extend compassion to others is limited by the depth of our self-compassion, and our ability to instil trust in others is fundamentally rooted in our capacity to trust ourselves. Moreover, increasing mastery of the art of leading from the inside out has transformed my confidence and ability to rise above setbacks with greater sensitivity and equanimity.

Creating Sustainable Change

My motivation to make a positive impact on the world has attuned me to opportunities to align my purpose with broader societal and environmental objectives, and I have been blessed by the number of opportunities to contribute to national change that have come my way. I've realised that while individual change is essential, it's collective action that brings about real transformation as diverse perspectives foster creativity, innovation, and a shared commitment to sustainable impact, especially in the context of complex social policy change.

I've found the qualities of True North leadership, clarity of purpose, clear values and the ability to lead from the inside out, have been vital to creating an environment in which people with competing agendas can come together, rise above their differences, and collaborate for the common good. Such leaders demonstrate insight; a future focus; the emotional intelligence to understand and manage human dynamics; respect for differing perspectives; and resilience to persevere through disruption and uncertainty.

Leaving a Lasting Legacy

I am humbled by the experiences that have shaped me and the impact I've been able to make as I reflect on my journey and recognise that my True North orientation has been a guiding force through the messiness of life. It has helped me deal with everything from challenging inequalities to championing environmental causes and helping individuals to develop their potential. Reflection on my journey toward purpose, profound insight, and the skills I need to make a difference has largely been unconscious and will continue for as long as I live. My True North qualities have evolved through a tapestry woven from personal experience, education, relationships, and work. Armed with this level of understanding, I know that acting more consciously is the key to interrupting current trajectories and accelerating positive change.

The way I see it, the journey to self-determination and self-fulfilment is about becoming aware of our developmental edge and consciously embracing the big, messy challenges that increase our courage and ability to effect positive change. Our ongoing development of self-leadership qualities is critical to our ability to realise our purpose. What I love is the fact that each day provides us with the opportunity to practise and strengthen these qualities. What I'm getting at here is that in a sense, our job as humans is to embrace growth, continue to develop our strengths, understand our thinking, and make sure our diverse impacts on others and the world around us are positive.

There's no doubt in my mind that True North thinking has underpinned my ability to create the certainty, focus, and power to thrive in chaotic times. That's why I decided to use this chapter to share some seminal experiences that deepened and transformed my insights and shaped my personal imperfect quest to "be the change you want to see in the world". As far as I'm concerned, this quote attributed to Mahatma Gandhi says it all.

I hope that what I've shared with you here will provide you with some insights and the knowledge that you have untapped potential that True North thinking and self-leadership can release. I'd love for you to do whatever you need to do to discover your unique gifts and use them to make the difference in the world you have been given the gift of life to make.

Warning: The process might release extreme joy, love and peace.

CHAPTER NINE

The World Doesn't Stand Still, Neither Should You!

Ben Newsome

Ben Newsome founded Fizzics Education in 2004 to deliver science education across Australia, having now reached 3 million kids. He is a qualified science teacher, 2013 Churchill Fellow, 2020 AMP Tomorrow Maker, the winner of the Australia small Business Awards a number of times, and the receiver of several Pinnacle Awards from the Center for Interactive Learning & Collaboration. Ben is a board member of 'Educating for Leadership', a past president of the 'International Society for Technology in Education Interactive Video Conferencing PLN', and is also the author of *Be Amazing! How to teach science the way primary kids love* and the host of the 'FizzicsEd Podcast'.

You can contact Ben at
www.fizzicseducation.com.au
linkedin.com/in/ben-newsome-cf-frsa-03169734

As you think over what you've seen happen over the years, the big things, the small things, the in between things – no matter what you've experienced, very few things have remained constant. In reality, the only thing that has remained constant is change! It doesn't matter whether you think about past world events, what's happened in your previous roles, or even in your personal life, change is inevitable. The good news is that we can always find serious opportunities to grow.

As I reflect on the changes I've seen in my professional life as an educator, the world has certainly changed since we entered the new millennium. Going back a bit further, social media didn't exist 30 years ago. Cloud computing was rudimentary, artificial intelligence was nothing like we're seeing now, and the spread of 3D printing, learning management systems, virtual and augmented reality, and the like were yet to happen.

As these technologies came in, they were highly disruptive to the existing systems in schools. And with this situation came friction. With a quick internet search, it doesn't take much effort to uncover the tensions that new technologies were bringing to classrooms. The tensions were articulated in the kinds of questions and the comments below:

- Do we have time to adopt this new technology?
- Even if we do have the time, what learning benefit would this new technology produce?
- What might be the unintended consequences of adoption?
- Do we have the budget for this?
- Do we have support systems in place to manage onboarding of staff, students and parents as required?

- But the old way still works!

From these tensions, I've seen several camps emerge within the education sector. Their existence is marked by:

- Widespread continual adoption of the new technologies following trials.
- Tentative adoption of technologies in small subsets of students or classrooms without being integrated widely.
- Inability to adopt new technologies due to budgetary constraints.
- Resistance to the new technologies regardless of the budget situation.

When you think about the differences in these camps, it's no wonder the adoption of technology across schools over the years has varied so dramatically. The differences weren't as noticeable prior to the Covid-19 pandemic, however with the onset of the global events of March 2020 onwards, it's easy to see why some schools were able to rapidly adapt to the changing environment whilst others struggled with the massive shift that was needed to move to online models of education.

Delays in adopting technological solutions when we went into lockdown arrangements were not just about budget constraints. In some schools it was the culture towards change that determined the success of the shift to online learning. I can't help wondering how the students in the schools that had been resistant to technological change would have fared if they were enrolled in one of the schools that was more responsive to emerging technologies.

If you were to reflect on the organisation you're a part of, which camp would yourself place you and your colleagues in? The thing is that change is inevitable, and it doesn't just occur in the context of operationalising new technologies. People move to new roles, restructures happen, new collaborations form, economic shocks emerge, and sometimes entirely new methods that we need to adapt to are introduced at short notice. The other thing is that change will never stop.

As you evaluate your organisation's response to change, I want you to consider whether it falls into the camp of embracing change or resisting it. With many years of experience in the education space, it's clear to me that an organisation's ability to respond to emerging technologies, market shifts, and evolving dynamics is matched by the degree to which it engenders a culture of adaptability, innovation, and continuous learning. These are the organisations that are better positioned to thrive amidst change. I say that because they are better able to seize new opportunities and proactively navigate any challenges that arise.

On the other hand, organisations that resist change are likely to find themselves struggling to keep up with the rapidly evolving landscape. They may face difficulties in adapting to new methodologies, incorporating emerging technologies, and responding to market disruptions. This can impact not only the organisation's growth and success, but also the experiences and outcomes of its employees.

So, what are we to do? From where I sit it's about finding the opportunities in change. What I know for sure is that it's in accepting change and adopting a flexible mindset that is comfortable with change that makes all the difference. Below are some specific and tangible strategies you can implement across your organisation, or even apply to your own situation.

Create continuous learning initiatives by –
- Encouraging a culture of learning by allocating time and resources for professional development for all staff.
- Investing in training programs, workshops, and courses related to emerging technologies, market trends, and the development of a wide range of relevant skills.
- Establishing mentorship programs and encouraging knowledge sharing within your organisation.
- Emphasising the importance of staying updated on industry news and developments.

Produce clear communication and transparency in the channels for the distribution of information by –
- Fostering open and honest communication channels where your colleagues feel comfortable expressing their concerns and ideas.
- Sharing information consistently about upcoming changes, opportunities, and challenges.
- Explaining the rationale behind decisions and impending changes to create a sense of purpose and direction.
- Listening actively to employees' feedback and honestly addressing their concerns.

Adopt a future-oriented vision by –
- Developing and effectively communicating a clear future focussed vision.

- Encouraging your leadership team to articulate the need for change and aligning it with the overall vision of the organisation.
- Defining strategic goals and metrics that reflect adaptability and responsiveness to change.
- Providing a platform for your colleagues to contribute their ideas and perspectives on shaping the future of the organisation.

Establish cross-functional collaboration by –

- Encouraging collaboration across departments and teams to break down silos and foster buy in.
- Acknowledging and/or rewarding diverse perspectives.
- Establishing cross-functional projects or task forces to tackle specific challenges and explore new opportunities.
- Promoting knowledge sharing and collaboration through digital platforms such as team collaboration tools or internal social networks.
- Recognising and rewarding collaborative behaviours and outcomes.

Encourage agile and iterative approaches by –

- Implementing agile methodologies to facilitate quicker adaptation to change.
- Encouraging experimentation and risk-taking in a controlled environment.
- Breaking down large initiatives into smaller, manageable projects to facilitate rapid iteration.

- Celebrating the small wins by using them as stepping stones toward larger goals.

Create change champions by –

- Identifying and empowering successful individuals within the organisation who can inspire and guide others through inevitable transitions.
- Providing change champions with the necessary resources and authority to drive change initiatives.
- Recognising and celebrating the efforts of change champions and highlighting their successes.

Encourage scenario planning and future trend analysis by –

- Conducting scenario planning exercises to anticipate potential challenges and opportunities.
- Analysing and discussing emerging trends and their potential impact on the organisation.
- Encouraging leaders to participate in industry conferences, seminars, and forums to gain insight into emerging technologies and trends.
- Fostering a culture of innovation and experimentation to explore new ideas and possibilities.

Apply resilience and adaptability training by –

- Providing training programs for staff focused on building resilience, adaptability, and a growth mindset.
- Offering workshops or coaching sessions on change management, including techniques to manage resistance to change.
- Celebrating examples of resilience and adaptability within the organisation to inspire others.

Recognising the inevitability of change and assessing the organisation's stance towards it can serve as a catalyst for growth and improvement. By fostering a culture that embraces change, encourages innovation, and cultivates a growth mindset, organisations position themselves to thrive in the face of ongoing transformation and emerge stronger and more resilient.

Of course, these strategies are multifaceted and require significant and consistent effort to apply and maintain. It might be daunting for some of your colleagues whilst others will naturally gravitate towards this mindset. And yes, mindset is the key. You can read a chapter like this and try to implement these strategies, but without creating growth mindsets within your team, it is less likely to be successful. So with that in mind, here are strategies that you can use to help your colleagues adopt a mindset to effect change and respond positively to it.

Create a safe environment by –
- Fostering a psychologically safe workplace where individuals feel comfortable expressing their thoughts and concerns without fear of judgment or negative repercussions.
- Encouraging open dialogue and active listening.
- Appreciating diverse perspectives and creating opportunities for everyone to contribute to the change process.

Lead by example by –
- Demonstrating a growth mindset and a willingness to embrace change personally.

- Actively engaging in learning, adaptability, and openness to new ideas.
- Sharing your own experiences and challenges related to change and explaining how you overcame them.
- Being transparent about your own learning process and encouraging others to do the same.

Communicate the importance of mindset by –
- Clearly articulating the significance and benefits of adopting a positive and adaptable mindset in the context of navigating change.
- Explaining how a growth mindset can lead to personal and professional development.
- Illustrating the benefits of embracing change, such as improved problem-solving skills and increased resilience.

Provide context and rationale by –
- Helping colleagues understand the reasons behind the proposed changes and their impact on the organisation.
- Communicating the potential benefits of the changes, both individually and collectively.
- Addressing any concerns or fears about the changes by providing reassurance.

Empower ownership and autonomy by –
- Providing individuals with autonomy to make decisions and take ownership of their work and the change process.

- Delegating responsibilities and encouraging individuals to take initiative in driving change within their areas of expertise.
- Recognising and celebrating individual and team achievements in embracing change and taking ownership.

Offer support and resources by –

- Providing the necessary resources such as training programs, coaching, or mentorship to help colleagues develop the skills and knowledge required for the changing landscape.
- Offering guidance and support to individuals who may be struggling with the change.
- Creating platforms for knowledge sharing and collaboration to facilitate collective learning.

Celebrate and share success stories by –

- Highlighting the positive results of individuals or teams who have successfully embraced change and achieved positive outcomes.
- Sharing success stories through various communication channels to inspire others and create a sense of possibility.
- Recognising and rewarding individuals who demonstrate a growth mindset and actively contribute to the change process.

Continuously reinforcing a growth mindset by –

- Consistently championing the importance of a growth mindset and adaptability in various communications, meetings, and interactions.
- Incorporating mindset-related discussions into regular performance evaluations and goal-setting processes.
- Regularly revisiting and reaffirming the vision and goals of the organisation, and emphasising the need for an open and adaptable mindset to achieve them.

When it comes to a growth mindset, the benefits transcend the boundaries of occupation and workplace – it becomes a way of life as it impacts every part of who we are and the results we achieve. The concept of change permeates every aspect of our lives. It is continual and unstoppable. How we choose to respond to change plays a pivotal role in shaping our happiness and success. Rather than succumbing to fear and uncertainty, I firmly believe that it is far more fulfilling to approach change with excitement and a sense of possibility.

Embracing a growth mindset means recognising that change presents a world of opportunities and potential. It is a mindset that empowers us to view challenges as stepping stones for growth, learning, and personal development. When we have a growth mindset, instead of being paralysed by the unknown, we can cultivate an attitude of curiosity and optimism. It enables us to navigate the complexities of a rapidly evolving world with resilience and adaptability. It also enables us to stay ahead of the curve, proactively seeking opportunities for growth, and continuously acquiring new skills and knowledge.

What's more, with a growth mindset we become active participants in shaping our own destinies, seizing the possibilities that change presents, and leveraging them to our advantage and the advantage of those we are surrounded by. Ultimately, adopting a growth mindset is not just about achieving success; it is about finding joy and fulfilment in the journey. By approaching change with excitement and a willingness to embrace the unknown, we tap into our innate capacity to learn, evolve, and thrive in an ever-changing world.

Remember, embracing change is a continuous process that requires effort and time. It is not something that will happen overnight. I'd like to invite you to reflect on your own experiences and consider the positive outcomes that change has brought throughout your life. As well as acknowledging the instances where change has presented challenges, and recognising the opportunities that arose as a result.

The thing is that change is an inevitable part of life, but the empowering truth is that you have the power to effect massive change. We all do. So, choose it.

Over to you.

CHAPTER TEN

Keep Moving Forward

Debbie Small

Debbie Small is a business strategist, relationship builder, speaker, thought leader and a global SuperConnector who connects business owners with high-calibre business experts; and helps you build a better business with more focus and less overwhelm. As the Founder of the 'Empowerment Point Global Business Directory & Education Hub', Debbie works with business owners who are passionate about making this world a better place; and building their businesses with solid business foundations. She has created an incredible directory and community of connections with heart and soul who really care about their clients and are focused on finding solutions. Empowerment Point gives business owners the freedom of choice through strategic guidance and provides a safe and supportive network of like-minded individuals.

You can contact Debbie at
www.EmpowermentPoint.com
linkedin.com/in/debbie-small-business-growth

Being vulnerable has never been easy for me; however, I know that it's my vulnerability that helps others realise that all of us have stories that have shaped our lives and brought us to where we are right now. When I feel at my lowest, I think of my family and the horrific things they have endured to ensure that I am here today. This gives me the strength to 'Keep Moving Forward'.

My grandmother was one of the strongest people I know – she had to be to survive. My grandparents were Holocaust Survivors, and the words 'Keep Moving Forward' were the only words they knew. My grandparents found themselves in one of the most horrific wars in history and they fought for their family and themselves to save as many people as they could, no matter what race or religion they were. My family came from Poland and in the 1930s the Holocaust began. The Holocaust saw the genocide of around 11 million people; a number of these beautiful souls were my family and the families of many people I know.

Like so many of their generation, they bore witness to the darkest chapter of humanity. From the 1930s following Hitler's rise to power, until the end of the Second World War, the Nazi regime carried out a campaign including that of sustained anti-Semitic persecution that developed into a coordinated programme of mass murder. This genocide, known as the Holocaust, had around 6 million Jewish people and close to 5 million non-Jewish people in Eastern Europe brutally murdered under the orders of Adolf Hitler. Entire communities were shattered and even children were not spared.

The Nazis employed a range of methods to persecute innocent people. Individuals were forcibly removed from their homes, transported in cattle trains to death camps and subjected to shooting, starvation, and gas chambers, as well as other horrific forms of murder.

My grandparents luckily spoke fluent German and became part of the Underground Resistance saving as many people as they could. Their life and that of their family were at risk every hour of every day, and they constantly had to be on guard. What my grandparents went through and saw no human being should EVER! When we were kids, we used to ask my grandmother to share her stories. My mum soon stepped in and asked us to stop as she could see her mum getting very upset while recalling these horrific moments; my mum was scared that her mother would have a stroke or heart attack having to re-live these memories. So we stopped.

There are two stories that stand out for me. The first was my grandmother on her way to drop off a package at a block of flats when she bumped into a woman she knew. Without even a thought this lady started yelling at my grandmother, "How come I have to wear a yellow star and you're not wearing one?" With Nazi soldiers everywhere, my grandmother was terrified she would be found out. She quickly spotted two exits and told the lady to wait as she walked briskly out of one of them and ran home to my grandfather and said "we have to leave right now"; and they did.

In Nazi Germany, the yellow Star of David was a symbol Jews were forced to wear. The practice began in 1941 and spread through Eastern Europe as a means of identifying and segregating Jewish people, and served as a tool of persecution and discrimination, marking the Jewish people for various horrors.

I too feel fear, but I could never and would never want to know the fear my grandparents felt on a daily basis. This puts my fears into perspective very quickly.

The second story is so horrific that I am actually crying as I write this, but I think it's really important for future generations to know the past so it is NEVER NEVER repeated. History is there to teach us what we shouldn't do, as well as how we can change the world for the better together as a collective.

The Nazis assumed my grandmother was German because she spoke the language fluently. If they had even the slightest suspicion of her being Jewish, I wouldn't be writing this today. My grandmother had to stand and watch even children being murdered, and if she even lifted an eyebrow, she would have been shot straight away. In her heart she was screaming and crying because she wanted to save everyone. My grandmother was an incredible woman who saved many people and made it through the war to bring her family to start a new and a much better life in Australia.

My grandmother was tough because of her life experiences. Without even realising it my mother inherited her mother's strength, but she was gentler with us in a positive way. My mum has been through a lot in her life and still today has the biggest heart I know. My mother's boundless love and compassion taught us that humanity transcends race and religion. Thanks to her, I have friends worldwide and have been able to build a global business centred around 'people', and around building relationships where acquaintances have become cherished friends.

My grandmother and my mother, though vastly different in their approach to life, have sculpted my thinking. They etched into my heart the indomitable spirit of 'Keep Moving Forward'. It's this mantra that propels me forward, igniting my passion to make the journey easier for business owners around the world. The entrepreneur world is a place where we as a group can create, invent, collaborate, co-create and empower others to have much better and easier lives. No matter where you are in life or in your business, we are all navigating our way through different obstacles to create our dreams, and this is all very normal for all of us. The trick is to 'Keep Moving Forward'.

'Keep Moving Forward' is more than a mantra; it is a promise to honour their enduring spirit, to reshape the world with every step and to ensure that the past remains the past as a poignant lesson in the pages of history.

I firmly believe that parenting is the most challenging and significant role in the world, closely followed by entrepreneurship. This is why it is so important for us to support each other. Long hours and a bumpy ride are very normal; however, I don't want people going through what I and many others have gone through. I spent a long time thinking that I could do it all on my own and this has cost me time, money and much of my freedom. It cost me many sleepless nights and lots of hiding under the covers not wanting to face the world. See! All these emotions you feel as an entrepreneur and a business owner are totally normal.

So, why do we embark on this seemingly crazy journey? Well, it's not just our eccentricity that drives us—although a touch of madness might help! The real motivation lies in our stories, which have inspired us to create businesses that lessen the challenges others might face, making their journeys smoother and more manageable.

I often interact with business experts globally who are going through challenges in scaling their business or needing help in different areas of their business. They feel alone and they are not sure where to go for help. Many business owners can feel not good enough, not focused and not knowing the steps to take. I wanted to create a space where business owners can find and learn from leading experts globally; 'Empowerment Point Global Business Directory & Education Hub' is the global umbrella over leading experts and networking groups around the world where our members also share their education and events. What fills me with pride about Empowerment Point is our members, they are all leading experts as well as great networking groups who have heart and soul and really care about their clients; we have an incredible directory of connections focused on finding solutions.

While we may excel in our specific domains, it's unrealistic to expect ourselves to have expertise in every aspect of business. Rather than attempting to tackle everything alone, I encourage business owners to tap into the wealth of knowledge offered by outstanding experts. Don't fall into the trap of trying to do it all on your own. My goal is to create a sense of community where business owners are surrounded by a supportive network of like-minded individuals.

So let me share some valuable business tips that have enriched my life throughout my journey. If you've read this far, I suspect something in my words has resonated with you and I hope these tips prove helpful as well.

- **Integrity:**
  Having integrity in life and in business is important. I have often had to make hard decisions that I didn't want to make as I was worried about how my members would see me. However, the decisions I make are with them in mind and what I believe is best for them. I will run this by my mentors and our executive team (built of our members) to ensure I'm doing the right thing. Having a great team around us is so important as they see things we don't always see, be kind to each other, look after each other and support each other.

- **Mindset:**
  The most important part of building your business is YOU. Your business is an extension of YOU and if you are not looking after yourself it's hard to look after the people around you; just like being on an airplane when they ask you to put your mask on first before helping others. So, the very first thing to focus on is your MINDSET. This can either make you or break you, and we definitely want it to make you! As our business journey is up and down, so is our mindset, and this is totally normal. There are and there will be plenty of times that you feel like you can't keep moving forward,

but you have to! Why? Because you have a dream to fulfil, you have a purpose, and because you want the freedom to be in flow and to live the life you truly desire; as well as to help who you want, when you want, how you want. There was a line I once heard that said 'how selfish is it for you not to share what you have learned when you know it can help other people'. I love this line and when I feel stuck, I often repeat it.

Your story, your experiences and your gifts have brought you to this point where you want to help others to not go through what you went through, be proud, be loud and share them. You never know who you are helping along the way. I have people who I didn't even know had read or seen what I put out tell me that I have made them believe in themselves or have helped them get out of a tough spot. Every time I hear this, I get teary and it's the motivation I need to 'Keep Moving Forward'. Take some self-care time for you every week, exercise, spend quality time with family and friends, and drink plenty of water through the day. Often, we are so busy that we forget how important these things are for our mindset. AND Laugh, laugh, laugh; laughter is like a magical potion that also gives our minds a break for a while.

- **Finance:**
  This is a big one as many entrepreneurs are so busy creating and thinking of helping their target market that they forget to keep their finances in check. Keeping your

finances in check will help keep you in flow, and help you be more focused and less stressed. Seek a great bookkeeper and accountant to help you keep on track and go over your finances weekly or at least monthly.

- **Creating your products and services:**
  The greatest ability an entrepreneur has is the ability to create. Create products and services that help your target market go from pain to pleasure, and provide them with the steps so that they don't have to go through what you went through. What entrepreneurs tend to forget is that these products and services also need to be sustainable to help them too. If you are undercharging you won't be able to help your clients long term as you won't have the money to Keep Moving Forward. Your clients and the people around you NEED YOU to 'Keep Moving Forward' and to keep helping them move forward. Remember when we create 'We are limitless by our imagination'.

- **Collaborations:**
  For those who know me know that I don't believe in competition in business, only in collaboration. As a team we learn from each other's experiences, stories and expertise to collaborate as well as co-create amazing solutions for our clients. We build ongoing relationships, and we share resources and our passion for wanting to make the lives of others easier and much

better. Collaborating also means that I get to work with amazing humans on a daily basis.

As I see what is currently happening around the world, my heart breaks. We must learn from history to have a great future. Learn from our mentors and those who have been there before us. It's up to our future generations to take the lessons of yesterday and turn this world into a place where acceptance of everyone is normalised and where decisions are made that will make this world a place where people can flourish through the goodness of others. I don't believe in competition I believe in collaboration; in business and in life we can work together to achieve so much more and truly light the way for others to have a much better future. If you believe you can, you can!

CHAPTER ELEVEN

Reimagining an Inclusive Future

Gloria Tabi

Gloria Tabi is the author of *Inclusive Teams & Workplaces: Everyone Wins!!* She wrote this book to assist leaders to become aware of the unique racial barriers faced by some of their staff, and how to improve their results by changing the systems, not the people. She established her business called 'EVERYDAY INCLUSION' to work with leaders to achieve inclusivity for their workplace. Gloria is passionate about helping leaders of all kinds to achieve workplace inclusivity that supports their people and future-proofs their businesses. She's helped countless leaders to achieve successful strategies for Diversity, Equity, and Inclusion, with over thirty-years of experience in providing proactive, tailored, and impactful training frameworks to ensure a safe, productive, and sustainable future for all.

You can contact Gloria at
www.everydayinclusion.com.au
linkedin.com/in/gloriatabi

I grew up in Ghana in Western Africa. I had no way of knowing how the advice an aunt gave me as I was preparing to migrate to Australia when I was 18 years old would play out in real time.

In Ghana, young people are encouraged to go to school and do their absolute best to achieve success at all costs. Looking back on it now, I can see how highly pressured life for a young child like me was. There was absolutely no room for error. It was a case of one strike, and you were out. For example, at the end of Secondary School, children in Ghana are required to sit an exam called the General Certificate Examination where there is only one chance to pass with good grades. Failure to achieve that cuts out any opportunity to do O-Levels which was the only path to get into university in those days.

Like all of the teenagers in Ghana in the 1980s, failure to transition to senior years would have resigned me to working in menial jobs on a farm or something like that. In this case, girls in particular were doomed to a future of menial work because they were not afforded the opportunity of apprenticeships like boys were.

Many young people internalised this pressure like I did. In my own case, I can see that the legacy of the pressure I was under in my formative years still impacts me to this day.

The background here is that Ghana was colonised for hundreds of years until 1957. By the time the British left, the country was decimated in terms of natural resources and human capital. Our resources were stolen including able-bodied men, women and children who were forcefully taken and shipped away to be slaves. While Ghana is an independent state now, the trauma of the past can still be felt. The sad fact is that it takes generations to rebuild a community that was so comprehensively pillaged.

I was definitely one of the lucky ones because I was able to migrate to Australia. This was something that most people only ever got to dream of. To this day I am incredibly grateful to have been the one who was saved from a life of destitution, hunger, illness, and poverty.

As well as being grateful when I was preparing to travel to Australia, I was also worried sick because I was leaving everything I knew behind. That included my family and friends. I remember feeling something that was very similar to the kind of pressure to succeed I was under at school. What's more, I felt like I needed to bottle up the fear and apprehension I was feeling so that I wouldn't come across as ungrateful.

The truth of it is that as a late teen I was terrified by the idea of leaving Ghana. Meanwhile, once the word got out about my good fortune there was excitement and celebration all around me. As very few of my extended family were able to travel to the city of Accra to see me off at the airport, a small gathering was organised for me to dine with those who could make it so that I could say goodbye in person. This was a great experience for me because I didn't get to see my extended family members often, and I relished the chance to bond with them before I left.

I remember this gathering vividly. It was September 1992. We talked, laughed, and cried about my imminent departure. In fact, I remember crying uncontrollably and feeling overwhelmed while listening to people saying things like –

"You are so lucky. This is a God-sent blessing. Your life is going to be so much better, and we are so happy for you."

One of my older aunts called Betty who had lived through the British rule in Ghana while she was growing up, said something that haunted me for a very long time. With kindness in her eyes as she gently touched my face she said –

"You're our beautiful princess, whatever you do, don't marry a white man."

Other members of my family encouraged me to listen to her. I heard what she said but I didn't fully understand where she was coming from at first. The conversation that followed left me in no doubt though. What she was reflecting in her words was a deep mistrust of white people. This was a part of the legacy of the British occupation in Ghana where colonialism decimated the culture.

Our culture is matriarchal. That means women have an important role to play in the way things are done. To my Aunt Betty and the others who were around the table when she shared her advice with me, marrying a white man would completely change the dynamic I would live my life through. Basically, they saw my move to Australia as an incredibly positive development, but they were worried about me losing connection to my roots.

I smile when I remember looking around at all of the white faces in the university I went to in one of the whitest parts of Sydney, wondering where on earth a Black African woman like me was going to find a suitable partner who lived up to Aunt Betty's expectations. To put it bluntly, the chance of meeting a Black African person from the Akan tribe in Australia was all but impossible.

Although my family perceived Australia as a land overflowing with milk and honey, it wasn't all plain sailing for me. In fact, it was a long way from that. Australia certainly had better opportunities like affordable access to university and good jobs, and it definitely had a much higher standard of living than Ghana, but as a Black woman I found myself subjected to racism on the streets and in the workplace on a daily basis.

I remember once when I was walking down the street, a white person walking towards me said (loud enough for me and everyone else to hear), *"You are trying to be normal dressed like that"*. I was taken aback and didn't know what to say. I just hurriedly passed him. Then moments later when I boarded the train I was on my way to catch when I was verbally assaulted about the way I looked, the family I sat next to gathered their belongings and went looking for another seat, apologising to others as they stumbled across the train to find somewhere else to sit. Nothing was said, but I knew they didn't want to sit next to me.

The first job I got in Australia was in a bakery. The only problem was that even when I was available to serve customers, most of them chose to wait for a white team member to serve them.

Fortunately, Australia is a lot more multicultural these days (although there's still room for improvement), but the experiences of my early days in this country I now call home continue to have an enormous impact on me in terms of the feelings of hopelessness and anger around the racism and prejudice I am still subjected to. The stains remain with me even now as a form of trauma that is embedded in my core. There was actually a time when I was scared to go out as a woman with Black skin in case someone decided to harm me. It wasn't just words that I was worried about either. The potential for being physically 'punished' for being Black was never far from my mind.

The kinds of experiences that embedded dread in my soul didn't end when I graduated from university with a degree. In fact, the only place I found solace without constantly being a target for the more overt racist abuse that was hurled at me was on the university campus. That was the one space where I truly enjoyed being in the early days of my life in Australia. I was able to meet new and diverse people, hang out, discuss ideas and topics of the day, and attempt to solve the world's problems like racism and environmental degradation with like-minded people.

Stable Square at the Richmond campus which was part of the university was my saving grace. It was a small space located on the very centre of the campus where bands would play on Friday nights. There were also festivals on Saturdays with stalls and a market like atmosphere, and church on Sunday. So, the university became a home away from home for me with some of my most beautiful memories of Australia being linked to my time there. University was a sanctuary where I could be myself. For a while, I could be in safety and amongst people who were genuinely happy to spend time with me.

Reflecting back on it now, there were (and to an extent still are) people in Australia who carry the legacy of colonisation like my parents and aunties did. What I'm getting at here is that exclusion, alienation, and racism are alive and well in Australia even to this day.

I am sharing so much of my story with you here because I believe we have a unique opportunity to direct the shifting sands the current environment presents us with. But before I enter into that territory, I want to reflect on the ways in which people from different cultures are fundamentally the same and joined by the common experiences of being human.

For me, maturing in a 'foreign' country complicated the desire to find a companion, a friend, someone I could trust. Feeling lonely and out of place, I remember how eager I was to meet someone I could share experiences with. I desperately wanted someone to laugh, cry, and just be with, without the constant concern about the colour of my skin getting in the way.

Australia was very different to the much more communal way of life back in Ghana. I guess that's why I gravitated toward group activities around the campus, and joined things like the International Student Association, the Student Mentoring Group, and the Christian Fellowship. In fact, this is how I met the man who became my husband and the father of my children. In case you're wondering, Dan is a white man. It was not an easy road to get to, it took six years after we met before we actually got married. During those six years there was a lot going on in the way of mindset shifts and expectations.

Reflecting on Aunt Betty's advice as I'm writing this chapter, I feel grateful for the privilege I was given to experience white culture. Through all of the uncertainty, discomfort, and downright suffering I experienced in the process of settling in, I can see the gift of the difficulties I experienced, and the way they've contributed to the fact that I've been able to go on and thrive.

The solution for me was to find ways to bridge a gap in my own understanding of racism and stay true to myself, while building enough confidence to challenge the status quo and reach out for help whenever I needed it. Getting to a place where I was able to decide that I wasn't going to let racism restrict my life gave me a real sense of purpose. I'm incredibly grateful for this because these days I get to work with wonderful people who are as passionate about the causes of diversity, equity, and inclusion as I am.

What I am suggesting is that as we make our way through the unusual times we're living in, there's immense value in staying open-minded and resisting the kinds of rigid rules that can restrict our creativity and connection with each other. While we heed the advice of our elders, it's important to place that advice within the context of the fact that the world has undergone a seismic shift, with things like blockchain technology offering alternatives to the way traditional financial institutions work, and world economies having been knocked around by the impacts of things like the Covid Pandemic, as well as worrying weather patterns emerging, and a level of political instability that has increased exponentially over the last few years.

The thing is that no matter what's going on around us, we all have humanity at our core, and if the instability we're experiencing can be used to move forward in a more inclusive way, then I say – let's bring it on.

CHAPTER TWELVE

Inclusive, Curious, Connected
– Building a Culture to Thrive

Annamaria Zuffo

Annamaria Zuffo has been teaching and leading in the ACT for 28 years, including being Principal at Lyneham Primary School for 9 years and now as Foundation Principal at Throsby School. High expectations and achievement for all students, regardless of their background, learning needs and circumstances, is central to her motivation as the Founding Principal of Throsby School. She believes that strong connections with self, each other and the land are central to students reaching their social, emotional and academic potential. She is a strong advocate for inclusion and social justice.

You can contact Annamaria at
annamaria.zuffo@ed.act.edu.au
linkedin.com/in/annamaria-zuffo-98144260

In 2021 when the world became more uncertain, I took a leap of faith and started questioning my philosophy as an educator of 26 years' experience, with 9 of those years spent as a Principal. The questions I reflected on were about:

What was most important to me?
What did I hold dear to me?
What were my non-negotiables?

So, I took the first leap ... and succeeded. I was blessed to become the Foundation Principal of a brand-new school that covers the critical preschool to year 6 period.

My values emerged from my reflections. The values in question were inclusion, curiosity and connection. That lead me to consider what I needed to do to build a school culture with these values at the core to educate young people with the skills and capacities they would need to go on and thrive. This is clearly a matter of global importance. I say that because people become the grown-ups they are as a result of the experiences they have when they are young, especially when they engage in formal and informal education.

In the realm of education, the role of a school principal is pivotal. Principals are not just administrators; they are leaders who shape the culture and environment of a school. I'm proud to say that I have been able to transform the educational experience for students, teachers, and the entire school community. I've been able to do this because I am a principal who is committed to fostering a positive school culture centred around the values of inclusion, connection, and curiosity.

This chapter explores the importance of these values and outlines a comprehensive approach for principals to cultivate them within their schools, and for leaders more generally to cultivate them within their teams. The thing I want to stress here is that before embarking on the journey of building the culture within any organisation, it is crucial to define the values that underpin its ethos. I'm going to talk about each of the values of my school in turn now.

Inclusion: Inclusion means welcoming and respecting the diversity of all students and ensuring that everyone feels valued and a part of the school community, regardless of their backgrounds, abilities, or differences.

Connection: Connection refers to the bonds that students, teachers, parents, and staff build within the school. This is about creating a sense of belonging, trust, and support among all members of the school community.

Curiosity: Curiosity is the engine of learning. It involves encouraging students to question, explore, and seek out knowledge. It's about nurturing a thirst for understanding and a love for learning.

Communication: The first step in building a positive school culture is clear communication. This is key to nurturing the values which should be prominently featured in the school's mission statement, vision, and daily operations.

The other keys to establishing and maintaining a positive culture are detailed below.

Professional Learning

Building a positive school culture requires a committed and skilled team. That's why investing in the professional development of teachers and other staff members to equip them with the knowledge and tools necessary to promote the school's values effectively is critical. This includes but is not limited to the following:

- Diversity and Equity Training: Offer ongoing training on diversity, equity, and inclusion to help teachers understand how to create a culturally responsive classroom and address bias if it occurs.
- The Curriculum: Provide training on inquiry-based learning and strategies to promote curiosity in the classroom, and encourage teachers to share best practices.
- Inclusive Teaching: Equip teachers with techniques to accommodate various learning styles and abilities, and create an environment where every student feels they can succeed.
- Restorative Practices: Develop a philosophy that emphasises a restorative approach that promotes understanding and reconciliation which will further foster the value of inclusion.

Student Engagement

To build a positive school culture, students must actively participate in shaping their educational experience. Ways to facilitate this include the following:

- Getting them involved: Encouraging their involvement in various aspects of school life will increase engagement and learning outcomes.
- Student Voice: Establishing a leadership group that gives students a voice in decision-making processes and their learning will increase buy-in.
- Extracurricular Clubs: Encouraging the formation of clubs and activities that align with the values of inclusion, connection, and curiosity will benefit the building of a positive culture. These clubs can be student-led and focus on community service, diversity awareness, and/or academic exploration.
- Peer Mentoring: Implementing peer mentoring programs where older students support and guide newcomers will promote a sense of connection and provide valuable role models.

Parent and Community Involvement

Building a positive school culture extends beyond the school walls. Actively engaging with parents and the broader community is the way to create a supportive network around your school. Ways to facilitate this include the following:

- Establishing a Parent Association: Encouraging parents to join the association and participate in school activities, as well as holding regular meetings to discuss the school's progress in fostering inclusion, connection, and curiosity will aid in embedding a positive culture in and around the school.

- Running Community Events: Organising events that involve the community including those that celebrate their children's learning achievements, as well as running workshops of various kinds will build connections between the school and its surrounding community.
- Engaging Guest Speakers: Inviting guest speakers from diverse backgrounds to share their experiences and insights with students can inspire curiosity about the world beyond the classroom.

Promoting Curiosity and Inclusion

To promote curiosity and inclusion, it's essential to develop a curriculum that aligns with these values. In addition to the points above, strategies to promote curiosity and inclusion could include the following:

- Providing Inquiry-Based Learning: Encourage teachers to incorporate inquiry-based learning into their lesson plans. This approach fosters curiosity by empowering students to ask questions and seek their own answers.
- Fostering Diverse Perspectives: Ensure that the curriculum includes diverse perspectives, voices, and cultures. This enables students to develop a broader understanding of the world around them and promotes inclusion.
- Focus on Real-World Applications: Connecting classroom learning to real-world problems and challenges not only sparks curiosity, but also shows

students the relevance and practical application of their education.

Conflict Resolution and Inclusion

In any community, conflicts will arise. So, it's crucial to have effective conflict resolution mechanisms in place to address issues related to inclusion and connection in particular. Strategies to facilitate this include the following:

- Maintaining Transparent Procedures: Develop clear and transparent procedures for addressing conflict, and ensure all members of the school community are aware of these procedures.
- Restorative Practices: Train staff in mediation and restorative practices that promote open dialogue and understanding, as well as encouraging students to participate in conflict resolution processes.

Celebrating Diversity

It is important for diversity to be celebrated as a strength within the school community because recognising and appreciating differences fosters a culture of inclusion and curiosity. Strategies to facilitate this include the following:

- Including Cultural Celebrations: Organise events and celebrations that highlight the cultural diversity within the school. These events can include things like food festivals, performances, and art exhibitions.
- Providing Access to Diverse Literature and Media: Ensured that the school library and classroom materials represent a wide range of perspectives and cultures.

This exposes students to different worldviews and encourages curiosity about other cultures.

- Nurturing a Multilingual Environment: Embrace multilingualism within the school by celebrating and supporting students who speak languages other than the primary language of instruction.

Mentorship Programs

Mentorship programs can play a significant role in building connections and fostering a positive school culture. At our school we provide peer mentoring programs where older students mentor younger ones in relationships that can provide emotional support and guidance.

Feedback Mechanisms

To continuously improve the school culture, it's essential to gather feedback from all stakeholders. Ways to facilitate this include the following:

- Surveys: Conduct regular surveys among students, parents, and staff to assess their perception of the school's culture, and use this feedback to make informed adjustments.
- Focus Groups: Organise focus groups to delve deeper into specific aspects of school culture. These discussions can uncover valuable insights and suggestions for improvement.

Leading by Example

The principal plays a central role in shaping the school culture. To be effective, they must lead by example. I like to think I do this well, and I'm proud to have established a team built around trust that enables me to do this. Strategies to ensure you are known as a leader who leads by example include the following:

- Modelling Consistent Behaviour: Demonstrate the values of inclusion, connection, and curiosity in all interactions you have with your fellow teachers and students alike, and in the way you make and communicate decisions. Consistency is key to building trust and credibility.
- Maintaining an Open-Door Policy: An open-door policy enables students, parents, and staff to communicate their concerns and ideas directly to you. This kind of accessibility not only fosters healthy connection, but also enables you to be on the front foot when it comes to problems and/or opportunities.

Evaluation and Continuous Improvement

Building a positive school culture is an ongoing process. Being vigilant when it comes to regularly evaluating results and making adjustments when required is an essential part of building and maintaining a positive culture in and around your school.

Conclusion

Inclusion, connection, and curiosity are not just words; they are the pillars upon which a positive school culture is built. Principals who are dedicated to these values can create an environment where every student feels valued, connected, and motivated to explore their curiosity. I can say from firsthand experience that embarking on this kind of transformative journey has enriched the lives of all members of the community at Throsby school where I am the principal, including my own.

CONCLUSION

I don't know if you realise you are a very special person. I say that because in not only picking up this book, but actually reading it all the way through to the end, you've shown a real commitment to making a difference in the crazy, unparalleled world we're living in right now.

Essentially, you've earned your stripes when it comes to taking your place in the ever-growing group of change makers who are not prepared to settle for the status quo.

You might remember me talking about the world needing a new playbook of global leadership across the fields of culture, business, and education in the Preface. I'm incredibly grateful to the amazing authors who generously answered the call to offer their own inspirational stories from their area of expertise with a future focused lens to get the ball rolling.

I want to hand the baton over to you now and invite you to join my community of changemakers, firstly by sharing *Global Matters* with your connections and networks, and secondly by making sure your leadership behaviours reflect the way you value humanity. If there's one thing I know for sure as I get ready to send this book off to be published, it's that people matter, and your contribution in joining a global ripple of human centred leadership creating a future different to now will be very much appreciated.

I hope this book has helped you to find your grit and grace – it's the rocket fuel for new global leadership.

I'd love for you to let me know how these inspirational stories have influenced your personal drive and resolve.